Artificial Intelligence (AI) as a Co-Pilot: Supporting Autistic Physicians and Medical Students

AI and Autism in Medicine: A Guide for Practitioners and Students

Second volume of the series

Artificial intelligence in medicine

Book series directed by Dr. Giuseppe Rotolo

Dr. Giuseppe Rotolo

To the autistic doctors who, with their empathy and dedication, are lovingly caring for so many challenging patients. Thank you for your commitment and for all that you do

Dr. Giuseppe Rotolo

Disclaimer

The author, a medical psychotherapist, has written this book about artificial intelligence in medicine based on their expertise and research in the field. The opinions and views expressed in this book are solely those of the author and do not reflect the views or opinions of any pharmaceutical or electro-medical companies.

The author has not received any financial support, compensation, or other benefits from any pharmaceutical or electro-medical companies in connection with the writing of this book.

The information and opinions presented in this book are based on the author's professional expertise and a review of existing literature and research in the field of artificial intelligence in medicine. The author has made every effort to ensure the accuracy and reliability of the information presented, but the reader is cautioned that the field of artificial intelligence in medicine is rapidly evolving and new developments may have occurred since the publication of this book.

Dr. Giuseppe Rotolo

The Artificial Intelligence in Medicine Series

Dr. Giuseppe Rotolo

Index

Dr. Giuseppe Rotolo

Dr. Giuseppe Rotolo

Dr. Giuseppe Rotolo

The Artificial Intelligence in Medicine Series

Dr. Giuseppe Rotolo

Introduction to the book series

We are on the cusp of a medical revolution. Over the past decade, computing has transformed the healthcare landscape, making medical advancements more accessible and affordable. In the past year, artificial intelligence has accelerated this progress, democratizing access to medical care and pushing the boundaries of what is possible.

This book series on artificial intelligence in medicine is designed for healthcare professionals, IT experts, and patients who want to stay ahead of the curve. We are committed to training AI systems that are not only more effective but also more compassionate, empowering healthcare providers to deliver personalized care and patients to take control of their health.

I would like to extend my gratitude to the European and American colleagues who have contributed to this groundbreaking work, their tireless efforts and dedication have made it possible.

With great excitement, I am proud to introduce the first book in this series, a milestone in our journey to harness the power of Artificial Intelligence (AI) for the betterment of human health.

Dr. Giuseppe Rotolo

Introduction to the first volume

As we stand at the threshold of the 21st century, we are witnessing a revolution that is transforming the very fabric of healthcare. Artificial Intelligence (AI) is democratizing access to medical information, empowering healthcare professionals and patients alike with a powerful tool that promises to revolutionize our understanding of disease diagnosis, treatment, and prevention.

While there are valid concerns about the potential risks and challenges posed by this technology, the benefits of Artificial Intelligence (AI) in medicine are undeniable. By analyzing vast amounts of data, identifying patterns and trends, and generating insights that were previously inaccessible, Artificial Intelligence (AI) is liberating clinicians from the shackles of limitations, enabling them to provide more effective and personalized care to their patients.

As Artificial Intelligence (AI) continues to evolve and mature, it is becoming increasingly clear that its impact will be profound and far-reaching. From medical imaging analysis to treatment decision-making, Artificial Intelligence (AI) is poised to transform the very way we approach healthcare,

Dr. Giuseppe Rotolo

revolutionizing the way we diagnose, treat, and prevent diseases.

In this series of books, we will delve into the world of Artificial Intelligence (AI) in medicine, exploring its applications, challenges, and possibilities. We will examine the current state of the field, highlighting its progress, pitfalls, and promises. And, crucially, we will explore how Artificial Intelligence (AI) can be harnessed to improve health outcomes, facilitate more efficient care delivery, and enhance the patient experience.

Throughout this series, we will draw upon the expertise of experts in the field, incorporating insights and perspectives from leading researchers, clinicians, and medical professionals. Our aim is to provide a comprehensive and authoritative guide to the exciting and rapidly evolving landscape of Artificial Intelligence (AI) in medicine, empowering readers to navigate this new frontier with confidence and clarity.

Join us on this journey as we explore the vast potential of Artificial Intelligence (AI) in medicine, and discover how this technology is revolutionizing the way we approach healthcare.

Dr. Giuseppe Rotolo

Introduction to the second volume

This book is born from the firsthand experiences of autistic physicians who have successfully navigated the challenges of medical education and practice. Their journey to becoming

Dr. Giuseppe Rotolo

effective healthcare providers has been marked by both triumphs and unique obstacles. This volume explores how Artificial Intelligence (AI) is transforming medical education and practice, particularly for autistic individuals. From medical students to practicing physicians and paramedics, artificial intelligence (AI) is providing innovative tools to address the unique challenges faced by healthcare professionals.

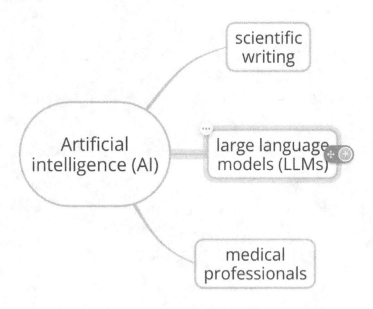

Individuals with autism often possess exceptional cognitive abilities, such as strong attention to detail and exceptional pattern recognition. However, they may also face unique challenges, including difficulties with working memory.

Dr. Giuseppe Rotolo

Working memory, the ability to hold and manipulate information in the mind, is essential for tasks like diagnosis, treatment planning, and medical research.

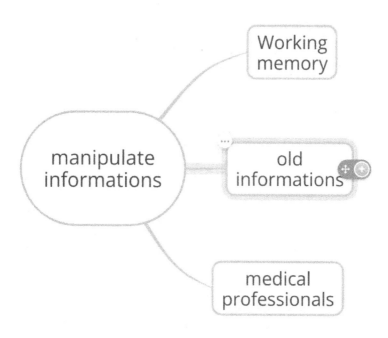

Artificial Intelligence (AI) can serve as a powerful tool to augment the working memory of medical professionals, particularly those with autism. By automating routine tasks, providing real-time information, and assisting with data analysis, artificial intelligence (AI) can help to alleviate cognitive load and enhance overall performance.

Dr. Giuseppe Rotolo

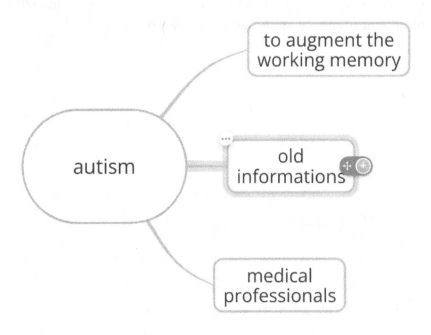

This volume explores how Artificial Intelligence (AI) is revolutionizing the way medical professionals, including autistic physicians, medical students, paramedics, and all healthcare providers, work, offering innovative solutions to the specific challenges they may face.

We will explore real-world examples of how Artificial Intelligence (AI) has transformed their practice, from diagnosis to patient care. Additionally, we will examine the broader implications of artificial intelligence (AI) for the

Dr. Giuseppe Rotolo

medical field and discuss the potential for creating a more inclusive and accessible healthcare system for all.

In our rapidly evolving digital age, Artificial Intelligence (AI) has permeated virtually every aspect of our lives, including the realm of healthcare. As the first volume in this series explored the broader applications of Artificial Intelligence (AI) in medicine, this second volume delves into a more specific and nuanced topic: the role of Artificial Intelligence (AI) in supporting medical professionals on the autism spectrum.

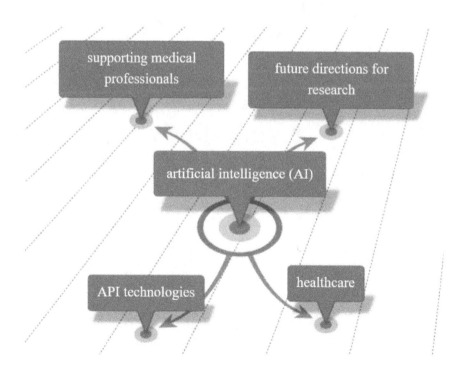

Dr. Giuseppe Rotolo

Individuals with autism often possess exceptional cognitive abilities, such as strong attention to detail and exceptional pattern recognition. However, they may also face unique challenges, including difficulties with working memory. Working memory, the ability to hold and manipulate information in the mind, is essential for tasks like diagnosis, treatment planning, and medical research.

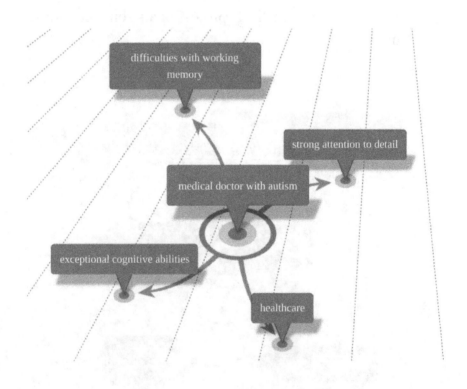

Dr. Giuseppe Rotolo

The Artificial Intelligence in Medicine Series

This book will explore the ways in which Artificial Intelligence (AI) can be tailored to the specific needs of autistic physicians and medical students. We will delve into the unique challenges faced by these individuals, and examine how Artificial Intelligence (AI) can be used to address these challenges and empower them to excel in their careers.

From diagnostic tools to treatment planning, we will explore a range of Artificial Intelligence (AI) applications that can benefit autistic medical professionals.

Dr. Giuseppe Rotolo

Parts of the book

Dr. Giuseppe Rotolo

The Artificial Intelligence in Medicine Series

This book examines the role of artificial intelligence in supporting autistic physicians and medical students. The first part provides a comprehensive overview of the unique experiences of autistic individuals navigating the complex world of medicine. By exploring the scientific literature, we delve into the specific challenges they encounter, from social interactions and sensory sensitivities to rigid thinking patterns. Despite these obstacles, autistic individuals often possess exceptional skills, such as attention to detail and strong logical reasoning.

The second part

The second part of this book focuses on how artificial intelligence can be used to support autistic physicians and medical students. We explore the potential of Artificial Intelligence (AI) to create a more inclusive and supportive healthcare environment. From Artificial Intelligence (AI) powered tools that can assist with communication and task management to data analysis algorithms that can help identify patterns in complex medical data, this book showcases the potential of Artificial Intelligence (AI) to enhance the abilities of autistic individuals and improve patient care. We will delve into specific applications of Artificial Intelligence (AI) in medical education, diagnosis, therapy, and research, highlighting how these technologies can empower autistic physicians and medical students to reach their full potential.

Dr. Giuseppe Rotolo

Part Three: Rebirth

The third part of the book continues to explore the role of artificial intelligence (AI) in supporting autistic physicians and medical students. It emphasizes the potential of Artificial Intelligence (AI) to transform the healthcare landscape and create a more inclusive environment for all individuals.

One of the key themes of this section is the importance of quality medical research. The authors argue that Artificial Intelligence (AI) can play a crucial role in improving the accuracy and efficiency of medical research, ultimately leading to better patient outcomes.

The book also highlights the importance of stress reduction for healthcare professionals. Artificial Intelligence (AI) can help to automate tasks and provide real-time support, reducing the workload and perceived stress of physicians.

Finally, the book calls for a commitment to creating a more inclusive and supportive healthcare environment for all individuals. This includes providing adequate training and support for autistic medical professionals, as well as fostering a culture of understanding and acceptance.

Dr. Giuseppe Rotolo

Professional commitment of autistic doctors

The inaugural chapter of this book commences with an exploration of several articles that illuminate the professional endeavors of autistic physicians. We initiate this exploration with a piece published in the esteemed journal Frontiers.

 Title: The experiences of autistic doctors: a cross-sectional study

Link: www.bit.ly/D-oc

Medical journal: Frontiers in Psychiatry

Date: 18 July 2023

As you can see, the article was co-authored by British and American researchers. I have also included the hospitals where my colleagues are employed to facilitate any potential collaborations.

Sebastian C. K. Shaw
Department of Medical Education, Brighton and Sussex Medical School, Brighton, United Kingdom

Dr. Giuseppe Rotolo

Alexander Fossi
Wendy Ross
Centre for Autism and Neurodiversity, Thomas Jefferson University, Philadelphia, PA, United States

Laura A. Carravallah
Department of Pediatrics and Human Development and Department of Medicine, Michigan State University, East Lansing, MI, United States

Kai Rabenstein
East Sussex Healthcare NHS Trust, St. Leonards, United Kingdom

Mary DohertyMary Doherty
Department of Neuroscience, Brighton and Sussex Medical School, Brighton, United Kingdom

Dr. Giuseppe Rotolo

Let's start by looking at the article together with a brief summary

This is a cross-sectional study about the experiences of autistic doctors. The study was conducted through an online survey distributed to members of Autistic Doctors

Dr. Giuseppe Rotolo

International, an online support group for autistic doctors. The study found that autistic doctors face many challenges in the workplace and many do not feel comfortable disclosing their autism to colleagues or employers. This lack of disclosure may be due to the fact that many autistic doctors have had negative experiences, such as bullying or discrimination, as a result of their autism. The study also found that autistic doctors have poor mental health, with high rates of suicidal ideation, self-harm, and suicide attempts. The study authors suggest that a neurodiversity-affirmative approach to autism may lead to a more positive self-identity and improved mental health for autistic doctors. They also suggest that providing adequate support and improving employer and peer awareness of autistic medical professionals may promote inclusion in the medical workforce.

Keywords of the article

For a quick view I provide the most frequent keywords in the article. Anyone who reads this book in electronic format will be able to appreciate the colors of the different keywords. Unfortunately the paper book is only in black and white.

Dr. Giuseppe Rotolo

Methods

Design: This research utilized a cross-sectional methodology. A participatory process informed the project's focus and the adaptation of a pre-existing survey to examine the perspectives of autistic medical professionals.

Dr. Giuseppe Rotolo

Data taken from the article

A total of 225 responses were collected. Among participants, 64% held a formal autism diagnosis, with a mean age of diagnosis at 36 years (range 3-61).

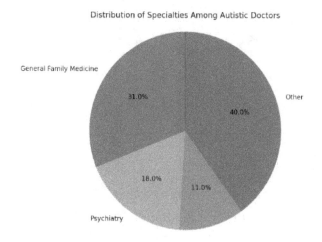

Distribution of Specialties Among Autistic Doctors

The majority (82%) were practicing physicians, primarily in general practice/family medicine (31%), psychiatry (18%), and anesthesia (11%). Nearly half (46%) had completed specialty training, while 40% were currently in training.

Dr. Giuseppe Rotolo

Disclosing an autism diagnosis to colleagues proved challenging, with 29% of participants reporting no disclosure. Although 46% had requested workplace accommodations, only half of these requests were fulfilled.

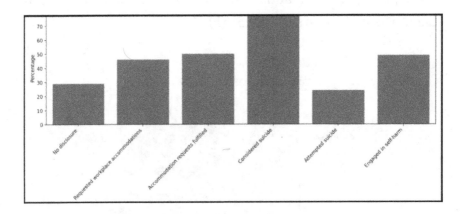

Mental health outcomes were severe: 77% had considered suicide, 24% had attempted suicide, and 49% had engaged in self-harm. Despite 80% reporting having worked with a suspected autistic colleague, only 22% confirmed working with a known autistic colleague. Notably, a lack of experience with potentially autistic colleagues correlated with increased suicide ideation.

The preferred self-descriptor was "autistic doctor" (64%), with most participants (83%) viewing autism as a difference rather than a disorder. Conversely, those who considered

Dr. Giuseppe Rotolo

autism a disorder were more likely to prefer the term "doctor with autism" and had a higher rate of suicide attempts.

Dr. Giuseppe Rotolo

Demographics and Experiences of Autistic Doctors

1. **High prevalence of autism among doctors:** More medical students and doctors are discovering they are autistic.
2. **Late diagnosis:** Many autistic doctors were diagnosed in their 30s or later.
3. **Common specialties:** General practice, psychiatry, and anesthesia were the most common specialties among autistic doctors.

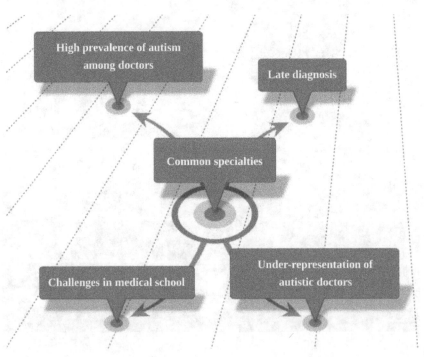

Dr. Giuseppe Rotolo

4. **Challenges in medical school:** Many autistic doctors reported difficulties during medical school.
5. **Under-representation of autistic doctors:** A significant number of autistic doctors felt their autism hindered their work.

Workplace Challenges and Discrimination

6. **Non-disclosure:** A large proportion of autistic doctors had not disclosed their autism to colleagues or employers.
7. **Lack of accommodations:** Many autistic doctors requested workplace adjustments, but only half were implemented.
8. **Discrimination and bullying:** Autistic doctors reported experiencing judgment, attitudes, and communication challenges from colleagues.
9. **Human resources and legal issues:** A significant number of autistic doctors faced HR or legal issues at work.

Mental Health and Well-being

10. **High rates of mental health issues:** Autistic doctors experienced high rates of anxiety, depression, and other mental health conditions.
11. **Suicidal ideation and self-harm:** A concerning number of autistic doctors had considered or attempted suicide.

Dr. Giuseppe Rotolo

12. **Impact of disclosure:** Disclosing autism to colleagues was associated with lower rates of self-harm.
13. **Benefits of support groups:** Membership in Autistic Doctors International was positively associated with mental health.

Autism and Identity

14. **Preference for identity-first language:** Most autistic doctors preferred to be called "autistic doctors."
15. **Autism as a difference:** The majority of participants viewed autism as a difference rather than a disorder.
16. **Impact of viewing autism as a disorder:** Considering autism as a disorder was associated with higher rates of suicide attempts.

Implications for the Medical Profession

17. **Need for workplace accommodations:** Creating inclusive workplaces with reasonable accommodations is crucial for autistic doctors.
18. **Importance of disclosure:** Supporting a culture of disclosure without fear of stigma is essential.
19. **Role of support networks:** Support groups like Autistic Doctors International can provide valuable resources and community.
20. **Neurodiversity-affirmative approach:** Adopting a neurodiversity-affirmative approach can improve the mental health and well-being of autistic doctors.

Dr. Giuseppe Rotolo

Conclusion of the first article

I conclude this article by addressing autistic physicians, medical students, and their patients. Becoming a doctor for an autistic individual is a deeply personal and rewarding journey.

Dr. Giuseppe Rotolo

While the path may be fraught with challenges, the ability to connect with patients on a profound level and provide compassionate care is incredibly fulfilling. Autistic physicians often bring a unique perspective to medicine, characterized by exceptional attention to detail and a strong sense of empathy. By overcoming the obstacles associated with neurodiversity, these individuals can offer patients a truly personalized and supportive experience.

Dr. Giuseppe Rotolo

Article by Dr. Mary Doherty'

Title: This Doctor Can: The autistic doctor

Link: https.bit.ly/D-o-

Author: Dr Mary Doherty

Now, we turn our attention to a personal account from an autistic doctor herself. Dr. Mary Doherty's insightful article offers a unique perspective on the challenges and rewards of being an autistic physician. Her experiences highlight the importance of understanding the individual needs of autistic medical professionals and provide valuable insights into the creation of more inclusive healthcare environments.

Keywords present in the article

Dr. Giuseppe Rotolo

Item description

This article delves into the experiences and challenges faced by doctors on the autistic spectrum. It sheds light on the social and sensory difficulties, anxiety, and depression that autistic doctors may encounter. The article also highlights the underdiagnosis of autism in medical professionals, which can lead to further complications.

Despite these challenges, the article emphasizes that autistic doctors can make significant contributions to the medical field. Their exceptional attention to detail, focus, and problem-solving skills prove to be invaluable assets. The article concludes by stressing the importance of support and understanding for autistic doctors, along with the need for further research in this area.

Dr. Giuseppe Rotolo

Here are some key takeaways from the article

Social and sensory difficulties: Autistic doctors may face challenges in social interactions, communication, and sensory processing. These difficulties can impact their ability to connect with patients and colleagues.

Dr. Giuseppe Rotolo

Anxiety and depression: The high-pressure nature of the medical profession can contribute to anxiety and depression in autistic doctors.

Underdiagnosis: Autism is often missed or misdiagnosed in medical professionals, leading to delayed support and interventions.

Strengths of autistic doctors: Autistic doctors possess exceptional attention to detail, focus, and problem-solving skills, which are highly valued in the medical field.

Importance of support: Autistic doctors require understanding and support from their colleagues and healthcare institutions to thrive in their profession.

Need for further research: More research is needed to better understand the experiences of autistic doctors and develop effective support strategies.

The article highlights the resilience and determination of autistic doctors who overcome their challenges to excel in the medical profession. Their unique perspectives and strengths can significantly contribute to patient care and the overall healthcare system. By fostering a more inclusive and supportive environment, we can empower autistic doctors to

Dr. Giuseppe Rotolo

reach their full potential and make a lasting impact on the medical field.

Dr. Giuseppe Rotolo

10 Key Points from the Article

1.   Autism is a condition that affects how a person communicates and interacts with the world around them.

2.   Many autistic people are highly intelligent and have exceptional skills in certain areas, such as pattern recognition and attention to detail.

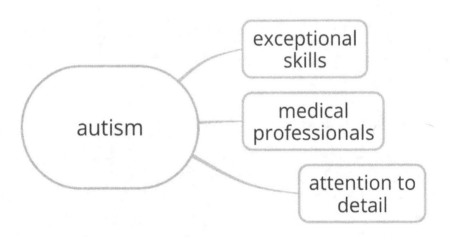

3.   Despite their strengths, autistic people often face challenges in social situations and may experience sensory sensitivities.

Dr. Giuseppe Rotolo

4.   There is a growing movement of autistic doctors who are advocating for increased recognition and support for autistic people in the medical profession.

5.   Autistic Doctors International (ADI) is an online support group for autistic doctors that provides information and resources to help them thrive in their careers.

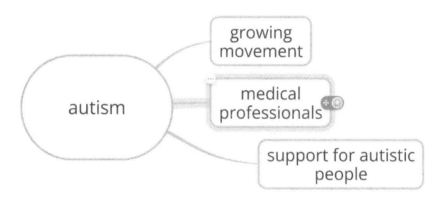

6.   Early diagnosis and support can make a significant difference in the lives of autistic people.

7.   Autistic doctors can bring unique perspectives and skills to the medical field.

Dr. Giuseppe Rotolo

8. More needs to be done to create a more inclusive and supportive environment for autistic doctors.

9. With the right support, autistic doctors can achieve great things.

10. Autistic Doctors International is a valuable resource for autistic doctors and their families.

The Lancet Psychiatry and The British Medical Journal (BMJ)

The first part of this book culminates with the inclusion of articles from two of medicine's most venerable journals: The Lancet Psychiatry and The British Medical Journal (BMJ).

Dr. Giuseppe Rotolo

These journals have a long and distinguished history of shaping medical thought and practice. Their inclusion in this book underscores the historical significance of research into the experiences of autistic doctors.

Dr. Giuseppe Rotolo

THE LANCET
Psychiatry

Title: Autistic doctors: overlooked assets to medicine

Publication date: April 2020

VOLUME 7, ISSUE 4, P306-307

Short link: www.bit.ly/th-e

Authors: Shirley Moore, Malcolm Kinnear, Louise Freeman

Panel: Lived experience commentary by Shirley Moore

Dr. Giuseppe Rotolo

Keywords present in the article

Dr. Giuseppe Rotolo

Short summary of the article

Autistic Doctors: Overlooked Assets to Medicine
This article discusses the potential of autistic individuals in the medical field. It highlights the unique strengths and challenges autistic doctors face, arguing for greater understanding and support to enable them to thrive.

Strengths of Autistic Doctors

Attention to detail: Autistic individuals excel at noticing and remembering minute details, which can be crucial in diagnosis and treatment.

Excellent recall: Their exceptional memory allows them to retain vast amounts of medical information, aiding in complex decision-making.

Creative problem solving: Autistic individuals often think outside the box, offering innovative solutions to challenging medical problems.

Passion and work ethic: Their strong commitment to their chosen field can drive them to excel in their medical careers.

Dr. Giuseppe Rotolo

Challenges Faced by Autistic Doctors:

Interpersonal difficulties: Social interaction can be challenging for autistic individuals, potentially hindering communication with colleagues and patients.

Executive functioning difficulties: Organization and planning can be difficult for some autistic individuals, requiring additional support.

Dr. Giuseppe Rotolo

Sensory sensitivities: Certain environments or situations can be overwhelming for autistic individuals, necessitating adjustments to their workspaces.

Masking and burnout: Trying to conform to neurotypical social norms can be exhausting, leading to fatigue and burnout.

Lack of understanding and support: Many autistic individuals experience discrimination or lack of understanding from colleagues, hindering their career progression.

The article emphasizes

The need for greater awareness and understanding of autism within the medical field.

The importance of providing support and making reasonable adjustments for autistic doctors.

The potential for autistic doctors to be valuable assets to medicine, contributing their unique strengths and perspectives.

Key Takeaways

Autistic individuals possess valuable skills and talents that can benefit the medical field.

Addressing the challenges autistic doctors face is crucial to maximizing their potential.

Greater understanding and support are essential for creating an inclusive environment where autistic doctors can thrive.

Dr. Giuseppe Rotolo

Conclusion on the article

The medical field stands to gain significantly from the inclusion of autistic individuals. Characterized by a unique cognitive profile, autistic doctors bring a distinct set of strengths that can revolutionize patient care. However, they often face significant challenges that hinder their full potential.

Autistic doctors excel in areas that are pivotal to medical practice. Their exceptional attention to detail allows them to meticulously analyze patient data, leading to more accurate diagnoses and treatment plans. Moreover, their remarkable ability to recall vast amounts of medical information equips them to make informed decisions even in complex cases. This, coupled with their often unconventional thinking, fosters innovative approaches to problem-solving, potentially leading to groundbreaking medical discoveries. Their intense focus and dedication to their work are further attributes that contribute to their success in the demanding medical profession.

Nevertheless, autistic doctors encounter numerous obstacles in their career paths. Social interactions, a cornerstone of medical practice, can be particularly challenging for autistic individuals, impacting their ability to build rapport with

Dr. Giuseppe Rotolo

patients and colleagues. Additionally, difficulties with executive functions, such as organization and time management, can pose hurdles in a profession characterized by tight schedules and complex tasks. Sensory sensitivities can create a hostile work environment, affecting their concentration and overall well-being. To cope with societal expectations, many autistic doctors engage in masking, which involves suppressing autistic traits to fit in. This constant effort can lead to burnout and mental health issues. Furthermore, a lack of understanding and support from colleagues can exacerbate these challenges, creating a hostile work environment.

To harness the full potential of autistic doctors, the medical community must undergo a paradigm shift. Raising awareness about autism and its implications for medical practice is essential. Implementing accommodations, such as providing quiet spaces or flexible work arrangements, can significantly improve the work experience for autistic doctors. Moreover, fostering a culture of inclusivity and respect is crucial to ensure that autistic doctors feel valued and supported.

By addressing the challenges faced by autistic doctors and leveraging their strengths, the medical field can create a more diverse, innovative, and compassionate environment. Recognizing autistic individuals as valuable assets will not only benefit these doctors but also enhance patient care and drive medical advancements.

Dr. Giuseppe Rotolo

BMJ British Medical Journal 2004; 329

Shot link: www.bit.ly/-BMJ

Date: Published 25 September 2004

A brief summary

Title: Life as a Doctor with Asperger's Syndrome

In this article, Dr. David H. Bailey shares his personal experiences as a physician living with Asperger's syndrome. Asperger's is a developmental disorder that falls within the autism spectrum, characterized by difficulties in social interaction and repetitive behaviors, while maintaining average or above-average intelligence.

Dr. Bailey acknowledges the challenges he faced while pursuing his medical career due to his Asperger's, such as difficulties with communication, social interaction, and understanding non-verbal cues. However, he also stresses the unique advantages that come with his condition. For instance, he has a methodical and detail-oriented approach to patient

Dr. Giuseppe Rotolo

care, with a strong focus on providing precise and accurate information to patients.

The author discusses the stigma and misconceptions that are often associated with autism, and how these stereotypes have impacted his career. He recounts instances of being labeled as difficult or unapproachable, and of being overlooked for leadership roles due to misunderstandings about his condition.

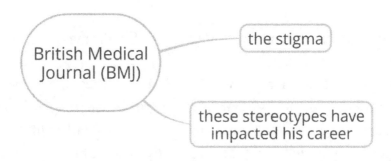

Despite these challenges, Dr. Bailey is a passionate advocate for the inclusion of neurodiverse individuals in the medical field. He believes that the diversity of thought and experiences brought by those with autism can enrich healthcare and improve patient care. He also emphasizes the importance of accommodations such as clear communication, structured work environments, and understanding supervisors to support the success of neurodiverse healthcare professionals.

Dr. Giuseppe Rotolo

In conclusion, Dr. Bailey's article serves as a powerful testament to the potential contributions of neurodiverse individuals in the medical field. It highlights the need for greater acceptance, understanding, and accommodations to ensure that everyone, regardless of their neurotype, can thrive in their chosen careers. The article ultimately encourages empathy, inclusivity, and the recognition of the unique strengths that each individual brings to the table.

Dr. Giuseppe Rotolo

The main keys of the article

Dr. Giuseppe Rotolo

20 Key Points from "Life as a doctor with Asperger's syndrome"

The author, Dr. David H. Bailey, was diagnosed with Asperger's syndrome. This diagnosis brought challenges and stigma, but also unique strengths to his career as a doctor.

Social interaction and communication were difficult for the author. This affected his ability to build relationships with colleagues and patients.

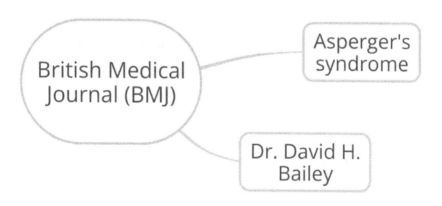

Dr. Giuseppe Rotolo

Sensory sensitivities made the busy hospital environment challenging. This included difficulty tolerating noise, light, and crowds.

Inflexibility and literal thinking created challenges in adapting to changing situations. This led to misunderstandings in communication and difficulty with ambiguity.

A strong focus and attention to detail made the author a meticulous and thorough doctor. He was highly organized and ensured accuracy in his work.

An excellent memory and ability to recall facts helped diagnose and treat patients effectively. The author had a vast knowledge base and could easily retrieve relevant information.

Honest and straightforward communication fostered trust with patients. The author's direct communication style was appreciated by patients who valued clarity.

The author advocates for increased understanding and acceptance of individuals with Asperger's in the workplace. He believes that neurodiversity can enrich healthcare.

The article highlights the need for awareness and support for individuals with Asperger's in the medical field. This includes accommodations and structured work environments.

The author stresses the importance of empathy and inclusivity towards neurodiverse individuals. He believes everyone should be valued for their unique strengths and contributions.

The article challenges the stereotypes associated with Asperger's and autism. It emphasizes that individuals with these conditions can be highly successful professionals.

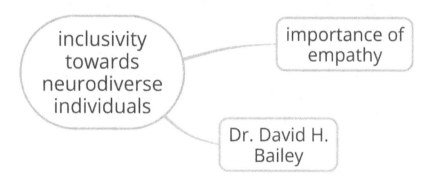

Dr. Giuseppe Rotolo

The author encourages early diagnosis and support for individuals with Asperger's. He believes this can help them reach their full potential.

The article sheds light on the importance of self-advocacy for individuals with Asperger's. It encourages them to speak up about their needs and advocate for themselves.

The author's story serves as an inspiration for others with Asperger's who aspire to careers in medicine. It shows that success is possible with determination and support.

The article raises awareness about the challenges and opportunities faced by neurodiverse individuals in the medical field. It encourages dialogue and understanding.

The author advocates for more research and resources dedicated to supporting neurodiverse individuals in healthcare. He believes this will improve patient care and create a more inclusive work environment.

The article highlights the importance of focusing on the strengths of individuals with Asperger's and other neurodevelopmental conditions. It emphasizes that these individuals can bring valuable skills and perspectives to the workplace.

Dr. Giuseppe Rotolo

The author encourages healthcare institutions to implement policies and practices that support neurodiversity. This includes providing training for staff and creating a welcoming environment for all individuals.

The article concludes by emphasizing that neurodiversity is an asset in the medical field. It encourages acceptance and appreciation of the unique strengths and contributions of neurodiverse individuals.

This article provides valuable insights into the experiences of a doctor with Asperger's syndrome, highlighting the challenges, strengths, and importance of inclusivity for neurodiverse individuals in the medical field. It encourages greater understanding, support, and appreciation for the contributions of individuals with Asperger's and other neurodevelopmental conditions.

Dr. Giuseppe Rotolo

Second part of the book

The first part of Artificial Intelligence (AI) and Autism in Medicine: A Guide for Practitioners and Students delves into the complex interplay between artificial intelligence and autism within the medical field. It underscores the distinctive challenges and assets of autistic physicians, advocating for the potential of Artificial Intelligence (AI) to bolster their professional journey. The text highlights the alarmingly high rates of late autism diagnoses among doctors, exacerbated by the dearth of understanding and accommodations during medical school and subsequent professional life. The book accentuates the disproportionately high prevalence of mental health issues within this demographic, emphasizing the imperative for comprehensive support and a neurodiversity-affirmative environment. Drawing on research from esteemed medical journals such as The Lancet Psychiatry and The British Medical Journal, the book provides a compelling case for increased awareness, inclusivity, and the strategic employment of Artificial Intelligence (AI) to harness the strengths of autistic medical professionals.

Dr. Giuseppe Rotolo

Chapter One

The Future of Healthcare: Artificial Intelligence (AI) and Autism

Dr. Giuseppe Rotolo

Empowering Autistic Physicians: Case Studies and Success Stories

Generative Artificial Intelligence (AI) offers a unique opportunity to create highly personalized interfaces tailored to the specific needs of autistic physicians.

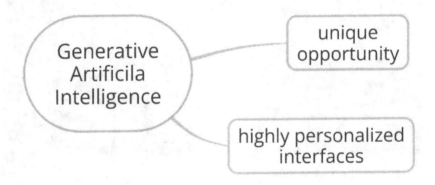

Dr. Giuseppe Rotolo

Strong personalization

The strong personalization of Artificial Intelligence (AI) used by autistic medical professionals can offer significantly improved performance, allowing autistic medical professionals to surpass the typical performance gap between autistic and non-autistic medical professionals. Indeed, with the use of personalized and in-depth Artificial Intelligence (AI), it's possible to achieve professional performance that exceeds the average.

Dr. Giuseppe Rotolo

This innovative interface represents a significant evolution in the way we access and retain information. Drawing on Richard Mayer's multimedia learning theory, these presentations offer a substantial advantage over traditional text-based formats by promoting long-term memory retention. Readers of the electronic version will benefit from the use of color-coded keywords, which provide additional layers of information and enhance comprehension.

This book, and others in the series, delves deeper into the concept of highly personalized Artificial Intelligence (AI) responses for autistic physicians.

Dr. Giuseppe Rotolo

We define personalization as the AI's ability to generate distinct and tailored responses to each autistic doctor, based on their individual needs, knowledge base, and query history. For instance, if one autistic doctor asks a specific question, the AI's response will be unique to that doctor, differing from the response it would provide to another doctor, regardless of whether they are autistic or not.

Dr. Giuseppe Rotolo

Personalization is tied to the learning style of each physician, regardless of neurodiversity. By tailoring Artificial Intelligence (AI) responses to accommodate for potential learning differences, including those associated with autism, we can significantly reduce cognitive load and enhance professional performance. This approach benefits all physicians, as it provides a more efficient and effective way to access information.

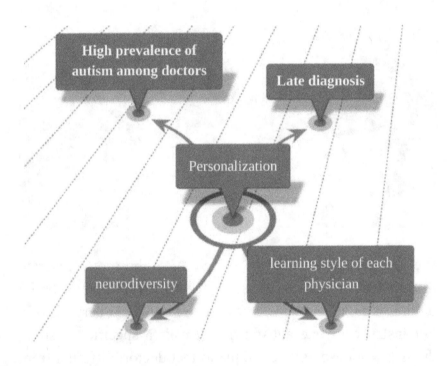

Whether a physician is autistic or neurotypical, individualizing Artificial Intelligence (AI) responses based on their unique learning style can lead to substantial

Dr. Giuseppe Rotolo

improvements in cognitive efficiency. By minimizing the mental effort required to process information, we can help all physicians optimize their performance and achieve better outcomes.

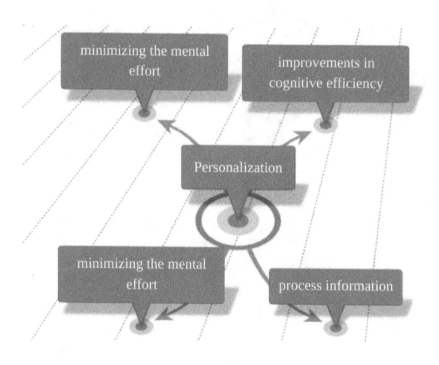

Personalization is an inclusive approach that can benefit all physicians. By considering the diverse learning needs of both autistic and non-autistic individuals, we can create Artificial Intelligence (AI) systems that are equitable and effective.

Dr. Giuseppe Rotolo

This approach not only reduces cognitive load but also fosters a more inclusive and supportive work environment.

Addressing the specific learning needs of each physician, regardless of neurodiversity, is essential for maximizing the potential of Artificial Intelligence (AI) in healthcare.

Dr. Giuseppe Rotolo

Tailoring Artificial Intelligence (AI) to Individual Learning Styles

- **Sensory preferences:** Beyond visual, auditory, and kinesthetic learning, individuals may have specific sensory sensitivities or preferences that can influence their learning experience. Artificial Intelligence (AI) can adapt the presentation of information to accommodate these variations, such as providing text-to-speech options or minimizing visual clutter.

How

Sensory preferences refer to the different ways individuals perceive and process information through their senses, which can include visual, auditory, tactile, olfactory, and gustatory modalities. Beyond visual and auditory learning, some people may have a preference for kinesthetic learning, where they learn best through hands-on experiences and physical activities. Others might excel in tactile learning, which involves using touch and manipulation to understand concepts. Recognizing these preferences can enhance teaching methods and learning environments, allowing for a more personalized approach that caters to diverse learning styles.

Sensory preferences: Beyond visual, auditory learning

- **Cognitive styles:** Different individuals process information in unique ways, such as analytically, holistically, or sequentially. Artificial Intelligence (AI) can adjust its approach to match these cognitive styles, ensuring that information is presented in a manner that is most easily understood.

Cognitive styles: Different individuals process information

How

Cognitive styles refer to the preferred ways in which individuals perceive, think, and remember information. These styles influence how people approach problem-solving, learning, and decision-making. For instance, some individuals may favor a more analytical approach, breaking down information into smaller parts, while others might prefer a holistic view, focusing on the overall context. Understanding these differences can enhance communication, teaching methods, and teamwork by allowing for tailored strategies that align with each person's cognitive preferences.

Addressing Cognitive Load and Enhancing Performance

- **Adaptive difficulty:** Artificial Intelligence (AI) can dynamically adjust the complexity of tasks and questions based on the individual's performance. This ensures that the physician is continually challenged but not overwhelmed.

Elaborate

Adaptive difficulty: AI can adjust complexity tasks

Adaptive difficulty refers to the ability of an AI system to modify the complexity of tasks based on the user's performance and skill level. This approach enhances user engagement by ensuring that challenges are neither too easy nor too difficult, which can lead to frustration or boredom. In educational software, for example, adaptive difficulty can help tailor learning experiences to individual students, promoting better understanding and retention of material. By continuously assessing user responses, the AI can dynamically adjust the difficulty, providing a more personalized and effective learning environment.

Dr. Giuseppe Rotolo

- **Contextual awareness:** By understanding the context in which a query is posed, Artificial Intelligence (AI) can provide more relevant and focused responses, reducing the cognitive effort required to search for information.

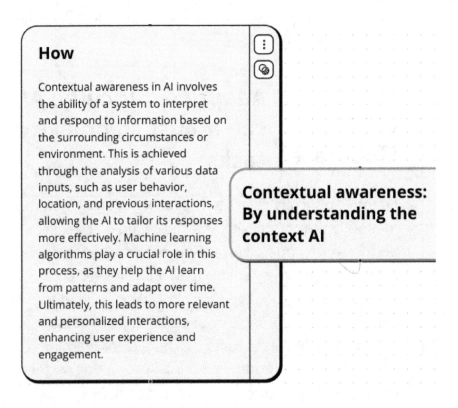

How

Contextual awareness in AI involves the ability of a system to interpret and respond to information based on the surrounding circumstances or environment. This is achieved through the analysis of various data inputs, such as user behavior, location, and previous interactions, allowing the AI to tailor its responses more effectively. Machine learning algorithms play a crucial role in this process, as they help the AI learn from patterns and adapt over time. Ultimately, this leads to more relevant and personalized interactions, enhancing user experience and engagement.

Contextual awareness: By understanding the context AI

- **Error analysis:** Artificial Intelligence (AI) can identify patterns in the physician's responses to

Dr. Giuseppe Rotolo

pinpoint areas where additional support or training may be beneficial.

Promoting Continuous Learning and Professional Growth

- **Personalized learning paths:** Artificial Intelligence (AI) can create customized learning paths based on the physician's knowledge gaps, career goals, and interests.

- **Just-in-time learning:** Artificial Intelligence (AI) can deliver relevant information at the precise moment it is needed, such as during a clinical encounter.

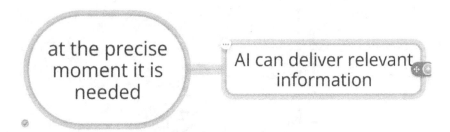

- **Collaboration and knowledge sharing:** Artificial Intelligence (AI) can facilitate collaboration among physicians, enabling them to share knowledge and learn from each other's experiences.

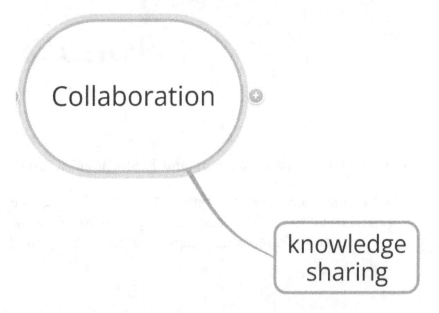

Example paragraph:

Dr. Giuseppe Rotolo

By tailoring Artificial Intelligence (AI) responses to individual learning styles, cognitive preferences, and performance levels, we can create a more personalized and effective learning experience for autistic physicians.

Dr. Giuseppe Rotolo

By reducing cognitive load and providing targeted support, Artificial Intelligence (AI) can enhance their ability to access, process, and apply medical information.

How

Reducing cognitive load involves simplifying information processing to enhance learning and retention. This can be achieved by breaking down complex tasks into smaller, manageable steps, allowing individuals to focus on one aspect at a time. Providing targeted support means offering specific guidance or resources tailored to the learner's needs, which helps them navigate challenges more effectively. Together, these strategies create an environment where learners can engage more deeply with the material without feeling overwhelmed.

reducing cognitive load and providing targeted support,

Furthermore, Artificial Intelligence (AI) can foster a culture of continuous learning and professional growth by delivering just-in-time information, facilitating collaboration, and identifying areas for improvement. These advancements have the potential to revolutionize medical education and practice, empowering autistic physicians to reach their full potential.

Dr. Giuseppe Rotolo

The Artificial Intelligence in Medicine Series

Dr. Giuseppe Rotolo

Quickly and intuitively

This technology can help to bridge communication gaps, reduce stress, and enhance the accuracy and efficiency of diagnoses and treatment plans. It's a promising development that could lead to a more inclusive and diverse healthcare workforce

Dr. Giuseppe Rotolo

By analyzing individual communication styles, learning preferences, and sensory sensitivities, Artificial Intelligence (AI) can provide tailored support. For instance, AI-powered tools could generate visual aids that are easy to understand, offer step-by-step instructions for complex tasks, and provide emotional support. Moreover, Artificial Intelligence (AI) can assist in automating routine tasks, allowing physicians to focus on higher-level cognitive functions. By addressing the unique challenges faced by autistic individuals, Artificial Intelligence (AI) can create a more inclusive and supportive healthcare environment.

By leveraging Artificial Intelligence (AI), we can create highly personalized tools that cater to the unique learning styles and needs of autistic physicians. By focusing on memory, comprehension, and data retention, Artificial

Dr. Giuseppe Rotolo

Intelligence (AI) can significantly enhance the professional capabilities of autistic individuals in the medical field.

Imagine an AI-powered platform that can:

Tailor information presentation: Artificial Intelligence (AI) can adapt the format and content of medical information to suit the individual's learning style, whether it's visual, auditory, or kinesthetic.

How

AI can adapt content presentation by analyzing user preferences, context, and engagement patterns. It utilizes algorithms to determine the most effective format—such as text, images, or videos—based on the audience's needs and the nature of the information. Machine learning models can learn from user interactions to refine these adaptations over time, ensuring that the content remains relevant and engaging. This dynamic adjustment enhances user experience by making information more accessible and easier to understand.

Tailor information presentation: AI can adapt format content

Enhance memory: Artificial Intelligence (AI) can use spaced repetition and other memory techniques to help individuals retain critical medical knowledge.

Enhance memory: AI spaced repetition memory techniques

How

Spaced repetition is a learning technique that optimizes the timing of reviews to enhance memory retention. It works by presenting information at increasing intervals, which helps to reinforce knowledge just before it is likely to be forgotten. This method leverages the psychological spacing effect, where information is more easily recalled if it is studied over spaced intervals rather than in a single session. AI can enhance this process by analyzing individual learning patterns and adjusting the review schedule dynamically to maximize retention based on the learner's performance.

Facilitate knowledge retrieval: By understanding the context of a query, Artificial Intelligence (AI) can

Dr. Giuseppe Rotolo

provide highly relevant and specific information, aiding in decision-making processes.

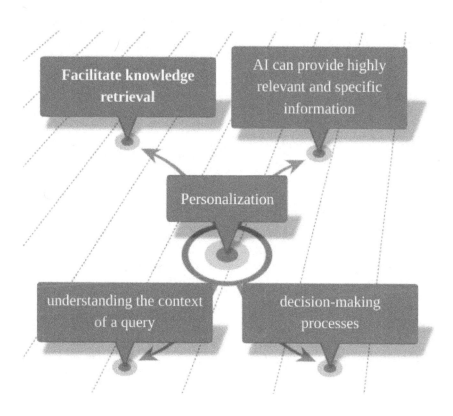

Integrate with existing medical tools: Seamlessly integrating Artificial Intelligence (AI) with electronic health records (EHRs) and other medical software can create a more efficient and streamlined workflow.

Dr. Giuseppe Rotolo

Furthermore, Artificial Intelligence (AI) can play a crucial role in promoting accessibility for autistic physicians. By offering customizable interfaces, providing clear and concise information, and reducing sensory overload, Artificial Intelligence (AI) can create a more inclusive and supportive work environment.

Dr. Giuseppe Rotolo

Chapter Two

A Different Lens: Seeing Autism Through a Doctor's Eyes

After exploring the foundations of artificial intelligence and its potential applications in medicine, it's time to delve into a personal experience that has shaped this work.

Dr. Giuseppe Rotolo

For over two decades, my career as a physician specializing in autism has allowed me to meet and collaborate with numerous exceptional professionals, many of whom are autistic doctors themselves. Among them, the story of one extraordinary individual has left an indelible mark on my memory.

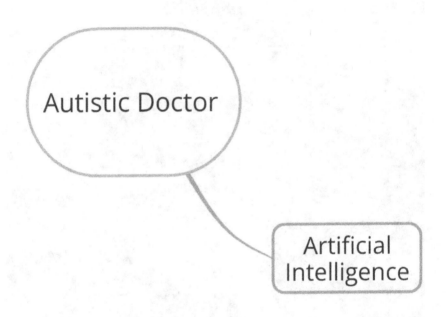

This autistic physician, after tenaciously overcoming the challenges posed by their condition, managed to significantly transform their symptoms and achieve a level of professional excellence. Their exemplary journey stands as a tangible testament to the extraordinary potential that resides within the autism spectrum.

Dr. Giuseppe Rotolo

But this is not an isolated case. Autistic Doctors International, an organization representing approximately 1000 autistic physicians worldwide, is a growing movement that challenges stereotypes and celebrates diversity in the medical field.

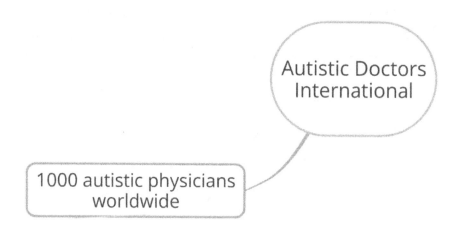

With this new perspective, the second part of this book aims to explore the experiences and achievements of these remarkable professionals. Through their testimonies, we will immerse ourselves in a world of resilience, ingenuity, and passion, where artificial intelligence emerges as a powerful tool to amplify their abilities and improve the lives of all.

Dr. Giuseppe Rotolo

Fatigue is a silent epidemic among autistic physicians

Fatigue is a silent epidemic among autistic physicians. Day after day, they navigate the complexities of their profession while simultaneously managing the unique challenges associated with the autism spectrum. From sensory overload to social interactions, autistic doctors often face a constant barrage of stimuli that can be exhausting.

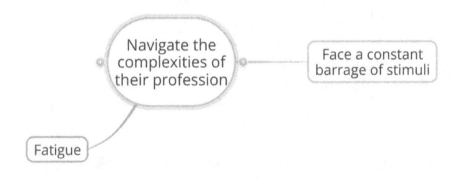

It's a relentless cycle: the need to meet the demands of their patients, the pressure to perform, and the constant internal struggle to mask their symptoms. But despite these challenges, autistic physicians continue to persevere, driven by a deep-seated desire to make a difference in the world.

Dr. Giuseppe Rotolo

The cognitive strain becomes unbearable

The cacophony of sounds intensifies, making it difficult to discriminate between voices. Words blur together, and the ability to comprehend becomes increasingly challenging. The

Dr. Giuseppe Rotolo

simple act of maintaining eye contact and engaging in conversation feels like an insurmountable task.

As the hours pass, a fog descends, clouding their thoughts. The ability to focus dwindles, and the once sharp mind begins to wander. Even the most routine tasks become arduous, requiring an immense amount of effort.

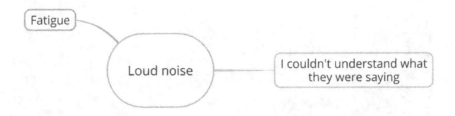

"*The loud noise of the hallway seemed to vibrate inside my head. Everyone was talking at once, and I couldn't understand what they were saying. My hands clenched into fists, and I wished I could disappear. The bright lights and unfamiliar smells overwhelmed me. I just wanted to go home*".

Dr. Giuseppe Rotolo

The cognitive strain becomes unbearable.

The cognitive strain becomes unbearable. The cacophony of sounds intensifies, making it difficult to discriminate between voices. Words blur together, and the ability to comprehend becomes increasingly challenging. The simple act of maintaining eye contact and engaging in conversation feels like an insurmountable task.

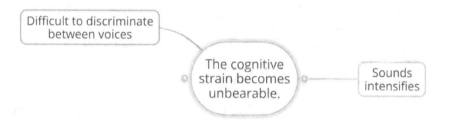

As the hours pass, a fog descends, clouding their thoughts. The ability to focus dwindles, and the once sharp mind begins to wander. Even the most routine tasks become arduous, requiring an immense amount of effort.

Dr. Giuseppe Rotolo

Personal connection

Autistic doctors often have a profound understanding of the challenges faced by patients with neurodevelopmental disorders, having experienced many of these challenges firsthand.

Dr. Giuseppe Rotolo

This personal connection allows them to provide empathetic and patient-centered care.

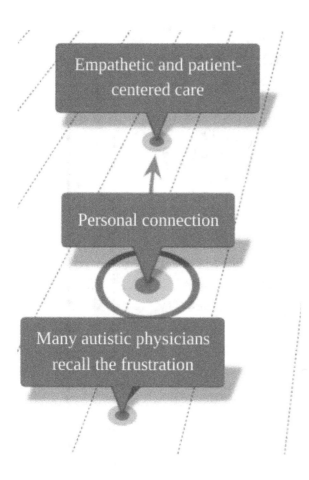

Many autistic physicians recall the frustration and despair they felt as children undergoing countless medical appointments, and they are determined to create a more

Dr. Giuseppe Rotolo

compassionate and supportive healthcare environment for future generations.

How **Many autistic physicians recall the frustration**

The concept revolves around the unique experiences and challenges faced by autistic individuals in professional settings, particularly in medicine. Autistic physicians may encounter difficulties in social communication, which can lead to misunderstandings with colleagues and patients. Additionally, sensory sensitivities might affect their ability to work in busy or chaotic environments, impacting their performance and job satisfaction. These factors can contribute to feelings of frustration, as they navigate a field that often prioritizes social interaction and adaptability.

Dr. Giuseppe Rotolo

The journey to becoming a doctor is fraught with challenges for anyone, but autistic medical students often face additional obstacles. Despite these hurdles, many autistic individuals are drawn to the medical field due to their desire to help others. Their unique perspectives and experiences can provide valuable insights into the patient experience, allowing them to offer innovative and effective treatments.

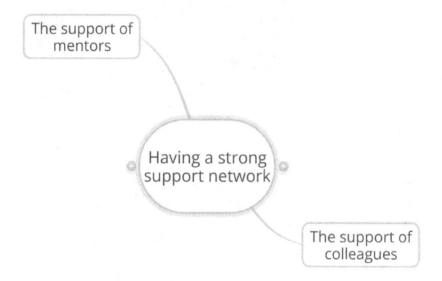

The support of mentors

Having a strong support network

The support of colleagues

The support of mentors, colleagues, and loved ones is crucial for autistic medical students and physicians. Having a strong support network can help to mitigate the challenges associated with autism and foster a sense of belonging within the medical community. By creating inclusive and supportive environments, we can empower autistic doctors to reach their full potential and make significant contributions to the field of medicine.

Dr. Giuseppe Rotolo

The eyes of the autistic doctor

As a child, I struggled with severe visual sensory overload. The world was often too bright, too chaotic, and my eyes felt like they were being pulled in different directions. Even the most mundane tasks, such as reading or watching television, were incredibly taxing. The constant strain on my eyes led to headaches, fatigue, and a general sense of discomfort.

Dr. Giuseppe Rotolo

Despite being diagnosed with strabismus, I believe there was much more going on. The visual therapies that I was prescribed were often ineffective and sometimes even made my symptoms worse. It wasn't until later in life that I began to understand the complexities of my visual experiences and the limitations of traditional eye care.

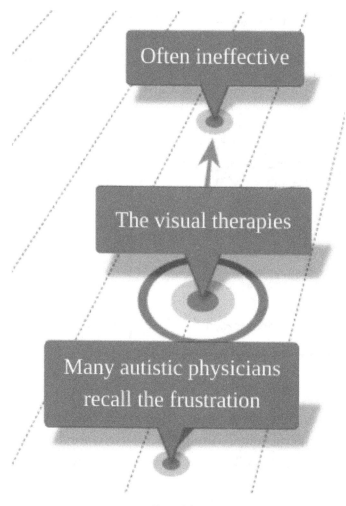

Dr. Giuseppe Rotolo

My visual difficulties had a profound impact on my daily life. I struggled to make eye contact, which often led to misunderstandings and social isolation.

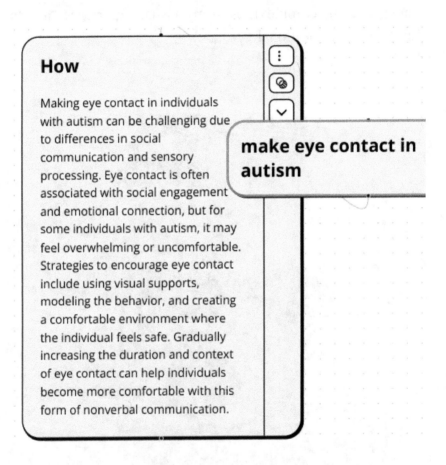

How

Making eye contact in individuals with autism can be challenging due to differences in social communication and sensory processing. Eye contact is often associated with social engagement and emotional connection, but for some individuals with autism, it may feel overwhelming or uncomfortable. Strategies to encourage eye contact include using visual supports, modeling the behavior, and creating a comfortable environment where the individual feels safe. Gradually increasing the duration and context of eye contact can help individuals become more comfortable with this form of nonverbal communication.

make eye contact in autism

The constant visual discomfort made it difficult to concentrate and learn, and I often felt overwhelmed by my surroundings. It wasn't until I found strategies to manage my

Dr. Giuseppe Rotolo

visual symptoms that I was able to function more independently.

For years, I was unaware that my perception of the world was so different. I've since discovered that I have synesthesia, a neurological condition where one sense is perceived as if by another sense. In my case, I experience colors as sounds. This unique way of seeing the world often led to misunderstandings and difficulties in school. I'd remember events as a series of auditory sensations rather than visual images, making it challenging to recall specific details, like the faces of my classmates.

The inability to accurately remember faces was a significant obstacle in my social development. I would often find myself in uncomfortable situations, unable to recognize people I had met before. This made it difficult to build and maintain friendships. It felt like I was living in a constant state of déjà vu, never quite sure if I had experienced a particular event or not.

As I grew older, I became determined to understand my own mind. Through therapy and self-reflection, I was able to develop strategies for coping with my unique challenges.

Dr. Giuseppe Rotolo

Learning about neurodiversity has been incredibly empowering, and it has allowed me to embrace my differences and see them as a source of strength.

Hypotonia, or low muscle tone, was a constant struggle in my early years. I would often trip and fall, and my motor skills were significantly delayed compared to my peers. The combination of sensory overload and poor motor coordination

Dr. Giuseppe Rotolo

made school a particularly challenging environment. By the end of the day, I was exhausted and overwhelmed, and I struggled to make sense of the information being presented.

autismo The sensory noise in the classroom was overwhelming

How

In a classroom setting, sensory noise can significantly impact students, particularly those with autism. Individuals with autism may have heightened sensitivity to sensory stimuli, making them more susceptible to distractions from background noise, such as chatter, movement, or even the hum of lights. This overwhelming sensory input can lead to anxiety, difficulty concentrating, and challenges in social interactions. To mitigate these effects, strategies such as creating a quieter environment, using noise-canceling headphones, or providing designated quiet spaces can help support students in managing sensory overload.

Dr. Giuseppe Rotolo

The sensory noise in the classroom was overwhelming. It was as if my brain was trying to process too much information at once. The constant background noise made it difficult to focus on the teacher's voice, and I often found myself zoning out. It was like trying to listen to a conversation in a crowded room the more noise there was, the harder it was to understand what was being said.

My sensory sensitivities and motor coordination difficulties made it difficult to participate in group activities and make friends. I often felt isolated and alone. I longed to be like the other kids, but it seemed like I was always one step behind.

Poor eye-hand coordination and visual processing made it difficult for me to complete tasks that required fine motor skills, such as writing or drawing. When I tried to focus on my schoolwork, the sensory input from the room would become overwhelming, making it hard to concentrate. It felt like my brain was trying to process too much information at once, and I would often end up with a headache.

The academic and social challenges I faced as a child left me feeling isolated and inadequate. I often felt like I was the only one who struggled in this way. It was not until I was diagnosed with autism that I began to understand that my experiences were not my fault and that there were others who shared my challenges.

Origin

The concept of autism has its origins in the early 20th century, with the term "autism" first being used by Swiss psychiatrist Eugen Bleuler in 1911 to describe a symptom of schizophrenia characterized by social withdrawal. However, the understanding of autism as a distinct developmental disorder began to take shape in the 1940s. Pioneering work by Leo Kanner in 1943 identified a group of children who exhibited a unique set of behaviors, which he termed "early infantile autism." Around the same time, Hans Asperger described a similar condition, now known as Asperger's syndrome, which highlighted a different presentation of social and communication challenges.

Dr. Giuseppe Rotolo

As time went on, it became increasingly difficult to differentiate between the psychological and physical manifestations of their condition. Today, we might label it a learning disability, autism, or something else entirely. Behind these diagnostic labels lies the immense suffering of countless individuals and their families, many of whom have faced delayed or inaccurate diagnoses.

Over the years, it became challenging to separate the mental from the physical aspects of their condition. While terms like 'learning disability' or 'autism' might be used now, the underlying reality is that many people and their families have endured years of uncertainty and distress due to late or incorrect diagnoses. These diagnostic delays can have a profound impact on an individual's quality of life.

The blurred lines between the psychological and physical components of their condition made diagnosis a complex process. While terms like 'learning disability' and 'autism' are more commonly used today, it's important to recognize that many individuals and families have suffered due to delayed or missed diagnoses. Early and accurate diagnosis can be crucial for providing appropriate support and interventions.

Dr. Giuseppe Rotolo

Growing up, mercury thermometers were commonplace household items.

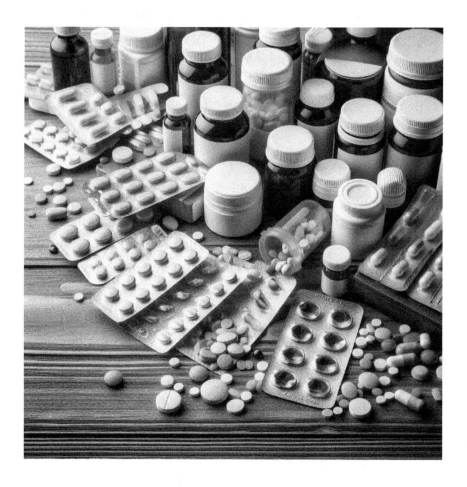

We were often fascinated by the silvery liquid and the way it moved. Little did we know that mercury is a highly toxic substance. Once a thermometer broke, the small, metallic

Dr. Giuseppe Rotolo

droplets seemed like harmless toys. However, as we've learned more about the harmful effects of mercury, it's clear that this casual exposure was extremely dangerous. The inhalation of mercury vapor can lead to serious health problems, including neurological damage. Some early studies have suggested a possible link between mercury exposure in childhood and the development of neurodevelopmental disorders like autism, although more research is needed to fully understand this complex relationship.

The widespread use of mercury thermometers in the past highlights the importance of ongoing research into the health effects of chemicals and the need for stricter safety regulations. Today, digital thermometers have largely replaced mercury thermometers due to their safety and accuracy. Parents and caregivers should always prioritize the safety of children and avoid exposing them to hazardous substances. While the exact causes of autism remain unknown, it's clear that early detection and intervention can significantly improve outcomes for individuals with autism and their families.

Dr. Giuseppe Rotolo

It's clear that many individuals, including yourself and your colleagues, faced significant challenges in obtaining a diagnosis for autism.

The lack of awareness and understanding of autism spectrum disorder in the past meant that many symptoms were often overlooked or misattributed to other conditions. It's

Dr. Giuseppe Rotolo

remarkable that many of you were able to make a self-diagnosis, especially given the limited resources and information available at the time. This speaks to the resilience and determination of individuals with autism.

The autistic doctor emphasized the importance of autonomy in their medical practice. This desire stems from the experiences of many autistic doctors who have faced discrimination and bias within the medical field. The International Association of Autistic Doctors has highlighted the need for greater understanding and acceptance of autistic professionals, who often possess unique skills and perspectives that can benefit their patients. By seeking autonomy, these doctors are striving to create a more inclusive and supportive work environment.

The autistic doctor's preference for autonomy is rooted in the experiences of discrimination faced by many autistic medical professionals. The International Association of Autistic Doctors has documented numerous instances of prejudice and bias within the medical field. By seeking autonomy, these doctors are not only protecting themselves from discrimination but also creating a more inclusive and supportive work environment. Their experiences highlight the need for systemic changes within the medical profession to ensure that all individuals, regardless of their neurodiversity, have the opportunity to contribute their skills and talents.

Dr. Giuseppe Rotolo

The autistic doctor described their secondary school experience as 'a disaster,' recounting how they were often marginalized due to their perceived 'strange' behaviors and perceived lack of competitiveness. Teachers, they explained, saw them as a student with limited potential, despite occasional flashes of brilliance that were quickly

Dr. Giuseppe Rotolo

overshadowed by the demands of a rigid, mediocre education system.

The autistic doctor described their secondary school experience as 'a disaster,' recounting how they were often marginalized due to their perceived 'strange' behaviors and perceived lack of competitiveness. Teachers, they explained, saw them as a student with limited potential, despite occasional flashes of brilliance that were quickly overshadowed by the demands of a rigid, mediocre education system.

The medical school journey, even for the most determined, was arduous and protracted. Yet, our anonymous interviewee's unwavering resolve to become a physician to help themselves and others served as a powerful driving force. Their ambition was not merely to practice medicine but to become a physician uniquely attuned to the often-overlooked disabilities of their patients. This individual envisioned a career path that prioritized empathy and understanding over fame and fortune. They made a personal vow to remain steadfast in their commitment to those who are least heard, regardless of the potential rewards or recognition that might lie elsewhere.

Dr. Giuseppe Rotolo

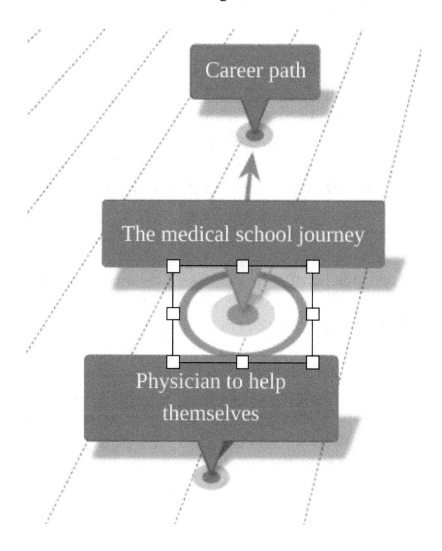

Dr. Giuseppe Rotolo

Sleep quality

In the final stages of our narrative, we delve into an often overlooked yet profoundly impactful aspect of life for many individuals with autism: sleep quality. Our physician, like many others, has long struggled with chronic sleep disturbances. Countless sleepless nights, frequent awakenings, and a persistent sense of fatigue have marked a significant portion of their existence. However, throughout their journey, they have achieved a pivotal milestone: significantly improving their sleep quality.

This accomplishment, beyond enhancing their overall well-being, has had a profound impact on their ability to navigate the challenges of daily life and excel in their academic and professional pursuits.

Sleep difficulties can manifest in various ways: difficulty falling asleep, frequent awakenings in the middle of the night, recurring nightmares, or superficial, non-restorative sleep. For many individuals with autism, these disturbances can be exacerbated by factors such as sensory hypersensitivity, anxiety, and difficulties with emotional regulation.

In the case of our physician, the causes of their sleep disturbances were multifactorial. Hypervigilance, a common trait in individuals with autism, made them particularly sensitive to any external stimuli, making it difficult to relax and fall asleep.

Additionally, concerns about academic challenges and social pressure could contribute to increased levels of anxiety and stress, triggering a vicious cycle of obsessive thoughts that disrupt sleep.

To improve their sleep quality, our physician experimented with various strategies. These included relaxation practices such as meditation and deep breathing techniques, adopting a strict sleep hygiene routine (going to bed and waking up at the same time every day, creating a relaxing sleep environment), and using dietary supplements and natural therapies.

However, it is important to emphasize that there is no one-size-fits-all solution. What works for one person may not work for another. Collaborating with a mental health or sleep professional can be crucial in identifying the underlying causes of sleep disturbances and developing a personalized treatment plan.

The story of our physician teaches us that even the most challenging obstacles can be overcome with determination and the right support. Their ability to improve their sleep quality is an inspiring example for all those struggling with this issue. It demonstrates that, with the right strategies and support, it is possible to achieve restorative sleep and significantly improve one's quality of life.

Dr. Giuseppe Rotolo

A good night's sleep is essential for optimal mental health and cognitive function. When we sleep, our brains consolidate memories, solve problems, and regulate emotions. Consequently, improving sleep quality can lead to enhanced cognitive abilities such as memory, attention, and decision-making. Additionally, it can reduce symptoms of anxiety and depression, and improve overall mood.

Dr. Giuseppe Rotolo

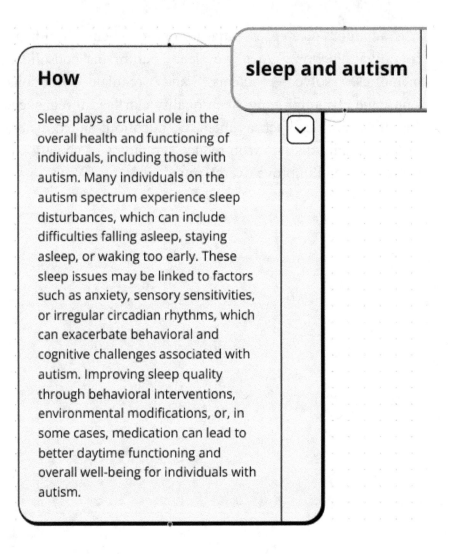

How

sleep and autism

Sleep plays a crucial role in the overall health and functioning of individuals, including those with autism. Many individuals on the autism spectrum experience sleep disturbances, which can include difficulties falling asleep, staying asleep, or waking too early. These sleep issues may be linked to factors such as anxiety, sensory sensitivities, or irregular circadian rhythms, which can exacerbate behavioral and cognitive challenges associated with autism. Improving sleep quality through behavioral interventions, environmental modifications, or, in some cases, medication can lead to better daytime functioning and overall well-being for individuals with autism.

Sufficient and high-quality sleep is crucial for peak performance. When we are well-rested, we have increased alertness, improved reaction time, and better problem-solving skills. This translates to enhanced productivity and a reduced risk of making errors.

Dr. Giuseppe Rotolo

Sleep is a fundamental pillar of overall health. Not only does it impact our mental and cognitive well-being, but it also plays a crucial role in physical health. Adequate sleep supports our immune system, regulates hormones, and aids in physical recovery. By prioritizing sleep, we can improve our overall quality of life.

Dr. Giuseppe Rotolo

Part three

Rebirth

The improvement was a process that spanned 30 years of dedicated study and therapy. The extensive years of medical
Dr. Giuseppe Rotolo

training allowed for a deeper understanding of the underlying physiological mechanisms involved, leading to the initiation of more effective therapies and a more accurate functional diagnosis.

Over 30 years of commitment to study and therapy, significant progress was made. Medical training provided the foundation for understanding the physiological processes involved, enabling the initiation of more effective treatments and a more precise functional diagnosis.

Subsequent to graduation, an encounter with colleagues specializing in functional medicine marked another pivotal juncture in my journey. Among these professionals were individuals dedicated to the study and treatment of autism. Their involvement with specialized autism hospitals provided invaluable insights and opportunities for professional growth. These experiences underscored the significance of a supportive professional network in navigating the complexities of autism spectrum disorder.

My personal and professional trajectories converged when I connected with colleagues specializing in functional medicine, many of whom were actively involved in autism care.

Their experiences working in dedicated autism hospitals provided me with a unique perspective on the complexities of the condition. These encounters inspired me to pursue further research and clinical work in the field of autism, driven by a

Dr. Giuseppe Rotolo

desire to contribute to improved outcomes for individuals on the spectrum.

The discovery of mitochondrial disorders, coupled with the analysis of urinary organic acids and the intricate world of the gut microbiome, has provided a profound understanding of the underlying causes of numerous perplexing symptoms. This wealth of medical literature has served as a beacon, illuminating the physiological pathways and biochemical imbalances that often elude traditional diagnostic methods. Through these advancements, we have gained invaluable insights into the interconnectedness of systemic health, revealing how dysfunctions at the cellular level can manifest as a myriad of clinical presentations. This knowledge has not only empowered clinicians to develop more targeted treatment strategies but has also offered patients a sense of validation and hope as they seek answers to their chronic health challenges.

After a decade of practicing functional medicine, the autistic doctor had significantly alleviated their own symptoms and those of many patients. Their professional performance had reached a commendable level. However, fatigue remained a persistent issue, far exceeding that of their neurotypical colleagues. It was an ongoing battle, a relentless pursuit without respite. The tasks were endless, and while therapies

Dr. Giuseppe Rotolo

proved beneficial, they were also time-consuming and seemingly infinite.

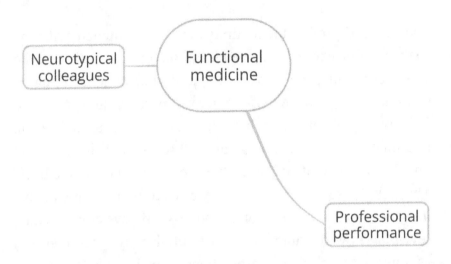

Ten years into their functional medicine career, the autistic doctor had made remarkable strides in managing their own symptoms and those of their patients. Despite these achievements, chronic fatigue continued to be a significant challenge. The demands of the field, combined with the persistent nature of many chronic illnesses, meant that there was always more work to be done. While therapeutic interventions provided relief, they often required substantial time and effort.

Dr. Giuseppe Rotolo

The Artificial Intelligence in Medicine Series

Over the course of a decade, the autistic doctor had become a highly skilled practitioner of functional medicine. They had successfully mitigated their own symptoms and those of countless patients. Nevertheless, the journey had been arduous, marked by persistent fatigue and an overwhelming sense of responsibility. Despite these challenges, the doctor's dedication to their patients remained unwavering, as they continued to seek innovative approaches to address complex health issues.

Dr. Giuseppe Rotolo

Game changer at last

In January 2023, a colleague introduced our autistic doctor to the world of free, publicly available Artificial Intelligence (AI). This encounter marked a radical turning point. Since then, the doctor's professional performance, diagnostic

Dr. Giuseppe Rotolo

accuracy, and therapeutic efficacy have soared. The ability to rapidly process vast amounts of information and conduct in-depth research with minimal effort has revolutionized their practice. Previously limiting symptoms, such as eye strain and a limited working memory, have been significantly mitigated."

A casual conversation introduced our autistic doctor to the potential of Artificial Intelligence (AI). This discovery has had a profound impact on their career. The doctor has been able to leverage Artificial Intelligence (AI) to enhance their diagnostic abilities, develop more targeted treatment plans, and overcome challenges associated with information overload. This technology has been particularly beneficial in addressing symptoms such as eye strain and limited working memory, which can be particularly taxing for individuals with autism."

The introduction of Artificial Intelligence (AI) to our autistic doctor's practice has led to significant improvements in efficiency and effectiveness. By automating many time-consuming tasks, the doctor has been able to devote more time to patient care. Moreover, Artificial Intelligence (AI) has facilitated rapid access to a vast array of medical literature, enabling the doctor to stay up-to-date on the latest research and develop highly personalized treatment plans. The

Dr. Giuseppe Rotolo

technology has also helped to mitigate the impact of symptoms such as eye strain and cognitive overload.

Example

Cognitive overload in individuals with autism can occur when they are faced with too much information or too many stimuli at once. For example, imagine a child with autism attending a birthday party. The environment is filled with loud music, bright decorations, and numerous people talking and moving around. This overwhelming sensory input can lead to anxiety and difficulty processing what is happening, making it hard for the child to enjoy the event.

As a result, the child might withdraw, cover their ears, or seek a quiet space to regain control. Strategies to help manage cognitive overload include creating a calm environment, providing breaks, and using visual supports to help the individual navigate the situation. Understanding these triggers is essential for caregivers and educators to support individuals with autism effectively.

autism cognitive overload

Dr. Giuseppe Rotolo

As Artificial Intelligence (AI) technologies advanced at an exponential rate, the autistic doctor committed countless hours to mastering their intricacies. With unwavering dedication, they explored AI's potential applications in medical research, diagnostics, and therapeutic interventions. This deep dive into Artificial Intelligence (AI) not only enhanced their clinical practice but also fueled their passion for innovation in healthcare.

Faced with the rapid evolution of Artificial Intelligence (AI), our autistic doctor embraced the challenge of becoming proficient in these technologies. By investing substantial time and effort, they were able to harness Artificial Intelligence (AI) to streamline research, refine diagnostic processes, and develop personalized treatment plans. This commitment has significantly improved both their efficiency and the quality of care they provide.

The ever-expanding landscape of Artificial Intelligence (AI) prompted the autistic doctor to embark on an intensive learning journey. Recognizing the transformative potential of these technologies, they dedicated themselves to staying at the forefront of Artificial Intelligence (AI) research and

Dr. Giuseppe Rotolo

development. By leveraging Artificial Intelligence (AI) tools, they were able to enhance their abilities in areas such as data analysis, pattern recognition, and predictive modeling.

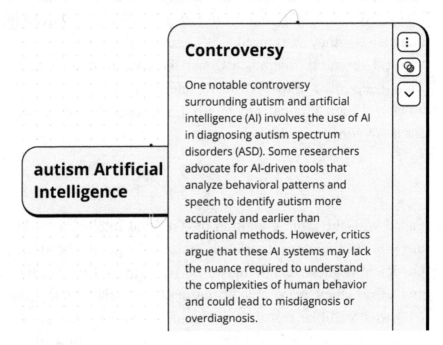

Controversy

One notable controversy surrounding autism and artificial intelligence (AI) involves the use of AI in diagnosing autism spectrum disorders (ASD). Some researchers advocate for AI-driven tools that analyze behavioral patterns and speech to identify autism more accurately and earlier than traditional methods. However, critics argue that these AI systems may lack the nuance required to understand the complexities of human behavior and could lead to misdiagnosis or overdiagnosis.

autism Artificial Intelligence

Artificial Intelligence gets better and better

As Artificial Intelligence (AI) technologies matured, a remarkable degree of specialization emerged. Within the medical field, a paradigm shift occurred as Artificial Intelligence (AI) systems were tailored to perform specific tasks with increasing precision. For instance, a cohort of Artificial Intelligence (AI) models was developed to efficiently scour vast databases of scientific literature, adeptly identifying high-quality articles relevant to a particular medical query. Simultaneously, another group of Artificial Intelligence (AI) models was designed to distill the essence of these articles, extracting key insights and summarizing complex findings with remarkable speed and accuracy.

This specialization extended to a myriad of medical sub-disciplines, with Artificial Intelligence (AI) systems being fine-tuned to address the unique challenges of each. The result was a sophisticated ecosystem of Artificial Intelligence (AI) tools, each contributing its unique capabilities to the diagnostic and therapeutic process. It became imperative for healthcare professionals, including our autistic doctor, to develop a nuanced understanding of the strengths and limitations of these Artificial Intelligence (AI) systems. The ability to select the most appropriate Artificial Intelligence (AI) tool for a given task and to interpret the results critically

Dr. Giuseppe Rotolo

was essential for maximizing the benefits of this technology and minimizing the risk of errors.

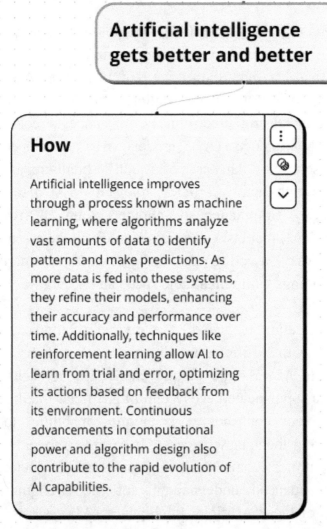

Artificial intelligence gets better and better

How

Artificial intelligence improves through a process known as machine learning, where algorithms analyze vast amounts of data to identify patterns and make predictions. As more data is fed into these systems, they refine their models, enhancing their accuracy and performance over time. Additionally, techniques like reinforcement learning allow AI to learn from trial and error, optimizing its actions based on feedback from its environment. Continuous advancements in computational power and algorithm design also contribute to the rapid evolution of AI capabilities.

Specialization: Artificial Intelligence (AI) systems were developed to perform specific tasks within the

Dr. Giuseppe Rotolo

medical field, leading to a high degree of specialization.

Efficiency: Artificial Intelligence (AI) significantly improved efficiency in tasks such as literature review and information extraction.

Accuracy: Artificial Intelligence (AI) models were capable of extracting key insights and summarizing complex findings with a high degree of accuracy.

Diversity: A wide range of Artificial Intelligence (AI) tools were available, each with unique capabilities.
Importance of understanding: Healthcare professionals needed to understand the strengths and limitations of each Artificial Intelligence (AI) system to use them effectively.

The advent of specialized Artificial Intelligence (AI) tools has revolutionized the pace at which scientific research can be conducted. With Artificial Intelligence (AI) automating tasks such as literature review and data analysis, the time required to publish a research paper has been dramatically reduced. Complex research projects that were once considered insurmountable for a single researcher, particularly one with autism, can now be undertaken with relative ease. As a result, the autistic doctor's output has increased exponentially, enabling them to consume and process a vast amount of

Dr. Giuseppe Rotolo

scientific information in a matter of weeks rather than months.

Through the use of AI-powered tools, the autistic doctor has gained the ability to rapidly acquire knowledge on a wide range of topics. By leveraging Artificial Intelligence (AI) to

Dr. Giuseppe Rotolo

summarize complex articles and identify relevant research, the doctor can quickly develop a comprehensive understanding of new areas of interest. This has enabled them to engage in meaningful discussions with institutions and experts, even in fields where they may have limited prior experience.

The integration of Artificial Intelligence (AI) into the autistic doctor's workflow has had a profound impact on their productivity and ability to acquire knowledge. By automating routine tasks and providing rapid access to information, Artificial Intelligence (AI) has enabled the doctor to publish research at an accelerated pace and to engage in interdisciplinary collaborations. This has not only expanded the doctor's knowledge base but has also allowed them to make significant contributions to their field.

What the autistic doctor had anticipated learning over the next two decades was being acquired in a mere year. This paradigm shift fundamentally altered their perspective, transforming them from a healthcare provider struggling to keep pace with neurotypical colleagues to a highly efficient and productive researcher. While certain symptoms persisted, the ability to accomplish a week's worth of work in a morning significantly mitigated the impact of fatigue, allowing them to focus on more strategic and creative aspects of their practice.

Dr. Giuseppe Rotolo

The doctor's learning curve had steepened dramatically. Skills and knowledge that would have taken years to acquire were now being mastered in months. This exponential increase in efficiency meant that tasks that were once time-consuming and arduous could now be completed with relative ease. As a

Dr. Giuseppe Rotolo

result, the doctor was able to devote more time to higher-level thinking and innovation, transforming their career.

The integration of Artificial Intelligence (AI) into the doctor's workflow had a profound impact on their career trajectory. By automating routine tasks and providing rapid access to information, Artificial Intelligence (AI) enabled the doctor to acquire the skills and knowledge necessary to become a highly productive researcher in a fraction of the time. This not only improved the doctor's quality of life but also allowed them to make significant contributions to their field.

Our autistic doctor bids us farewell with a serene smile, a ray of sunshine illuminating an often winding path. It is the smile of one who has scaled unimaginable heights, overcoming obstacles that many would have deemed insurmountable. It is the smile of someone who has found deep fulfillment in contributing to the well-being of others, using their unique abilities to make a difference.

Their journey is a tangible testament to the fact that diversity, far from being a limitation, can be a source of great strength and creativity. They have shown that with determination, passion, and the aid of the right technologies, it is possible to overcome the most daunting challenges and achieve extraordinary results.

Dr. Giuseppe Rotolo

Their smile reminds us that life, even in its darkest manifestations, always conceals a spark of hope. It is an invitation to never give up, to believe in one's own abilities, and to seek the good, even in the most difficult of times. Their story is a beacon that illuminates the path of those who, like them, feel different and seek meaning in the world.

Dr. Giuseppe Rotolo

This autistic doctor has taught us that happiness is not a destination to be reached, but a journey to be undertaken. It is a continuous becoming, a constant evolution. And they have shown us that even those who start from a position of apparent disadvantage can reach unexpected heights, helping to make the world a better place.

We hope that the world will soon evolve into a more inclusive society, where diversity is not only tolerated but celebrated as a richness. Imagine a future where autistic doctors and all neurodivergent people can fully express their potential, without having to hide who they are. Every individual, with their uniqueness, can contribute to creating a fairer and more compassionate world. Every hasty judgment that is suspended, every prejudice that is challenged, is a step forward towards a brighter future. In a world that accepts and values diversity, each of us can find our place and feel part of something greater.

It is our hope that institutions at all levels will commit to promoting inclusion and challenging stereotypes. Schools, universities, and workplaces must become welcoming environments for all, where diversity is seen as a resource. Investing in inclusive education is essential to building a more equitable and just society. Only through education can we eradicate prejudice and promote empathy, creating the

Dr. Giuseppe Rotolo

conditions necessary for a world where every individual can fully realize their potential.

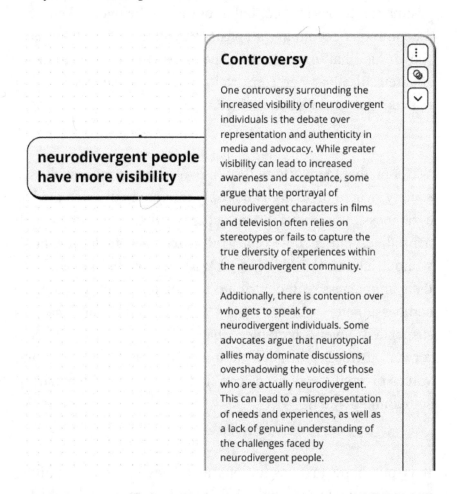

Controversy

One controversy surrounding the increased visibility of neurodivergent individuals is the debate over representation and authenticity in media and advocacy. While greater visibility can lead to increased awareness and acceptance, some argue that the portrayal of neurodivergent characters in films and television often relies on stereotypes or fails to capture the true diversity of experiences within the neurodivergent community.

Additionally, there is contention over who gets to speak for neurodivergent individuals. Some advocates argue that neurotypical allies may dominate discussions, overshadowing the voices of those who are actually neurodivergent. This can lead to a misrepresentation of needs and experiences, as well as a lack of genuine understanding of the challenges faced by neurodivergent people.

neurodivergent people have more visibility

It is important that neurodivergent people have more visibility and are represented in the media, culture, and politics. Having positive role models is essential for young people, especially those who feel different. When we see people like us who have succeeded, we understand that we can achieve our

Dr. Giuseppe Rotolo

dreams and that our differences are a strength, not a weakness. We hope that soon the social narrative will change and that the success stories of neurodivergent people will become increasingly common.

Dr. Giuseppe Rotolo

What is the moral of all this?

As we approach the conclusion of the second volume of this second series, we have only briefly mentioned the patents we are developing to make artificial intelligence more accessible, replicating the results achieved by our autistic doctor. In the next volumes, we will delve deeper into how Artificial Intelligence (AI) can collaborate with human researchers, both autistic and neurotypical, to overcome challenges in various fields. Imagine a future where Artificial Intelligence (AI) is not just a tool, but a true research partner, capable of analyzing vast amounts of data, identifying hidden patterns, and suggesting new hypotheses. This synergy between man and machine could lead to revolutionary discoveries in medicine, neuroscience, and many other disciplines.

Approaching the conclusion of this second volume, we have only briefly mentioned the patents we are developing to simplify the use of Artificial Intelligence (AI), inspired by the successes of our autistic doctor. In the upcoming volumes, we will explore in detail how different Artificial Intelligence (AI) can support the specific challenges faced by autistic researchers, such as managing sensory overload, difficulty interpreting non-verbal information, and a tendency to focus

Dr. Giuseppe Rotolo

144

on specific details. Artificial Intelligence (AI) could provide personalized tools to help these researchers make the most of their unique abilities and overcome any difficulties they may encounter.

Dr. Giuseppe Rotolo

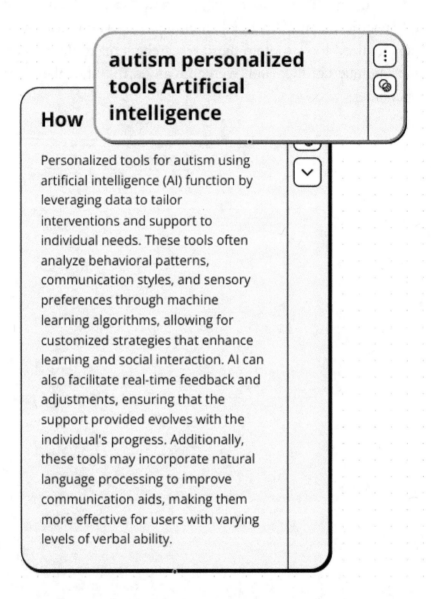

autism personalized tools Artificial intelligence

How

Personalized tools for autism using artificial intelligence (AI) function by leveraging data to tailor interventions and support to individual needs. These tools often analyze behavioral patterns, communication styles, and sensory preferences through machine learning algorithms, allowing for customized strategies that enhance learning and social interaction. AI can also facilitate real-time feedback and adjustments, ensuring that the support provided evolves with the individual's progress. Additionally, these tools may incorporate natural language processing to improve communication aids, making them more effective for users with varying levels of verbal ability.

As we conclude this second volume of the second series, we have only briefly mentioned the patents we are developing to make Artificial Intelligence (AI) more intuitive, replicating

Dr. Giuseppe Rotolo

the results of our autistic doctor. In the next volumes, we will examine how Artificial Intelligence (AI) can collaborate with human researchers, both autistic and neurotypical, to accelerate innovation in various sectors. Imagine a future where Artificial Intelligence (AI) not only helps researchers find solutions to complex problems, but also contributes to developing new technologies and improving the quality of life for millions of people. This synergy between man and machine could lead to an era of unprecedented discoveries and social progress.

As a physician who uses Artificial Intelligence (AI) in daily clinical practice, I have firsthand experience of how this technology is revolutionizing our field. Artificial Intelligence (AI) assists me in multiple tasks: from laboratory analysis for more accurate and early diagnoses, to creating personalized treatment plans based on genomic and clinical data, to managing patient data more efficiently. Particularly in the context of volunteering, where resources are limited and needs are often complex, Artificial Intelligence (AI) allows me to optimize my time, make more informed decisions, and offer high-quality care to a larger number of patients.

Artificial Intelligence (AI) is democratizing access to high-quality medical care. Thanks to AI-powered telemedicine tools, it is possible to provide remote consultations and diagnoses, even in remote or disadvantaged areas.

Dr. Giuseppe Rotolo

Additionally, Artificial Intelligence (AI) can help reduce healthcare disparities by providing decision support tools that take into account the specific characteristics of different populations.

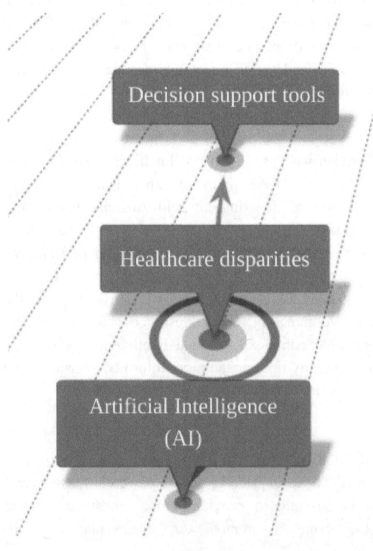

Dr. Giuseppe Rotolo

In my volunteer work, I have been able to experience how Artificial Intelligence (AI) can contribute to improving the health of people who would otherwise have difficulty accessing adequate care.

The integration of Artificial Intelligence (AI) into clinical practice undoubtedly presents challenges, such as the need to ensure data quality, patient privacy, and the correct interpretation of results. However, the potential benefits are enormous. I envision a future where Artificial Intelligence (AI) will be an indispensable tool for every physician, allowing us to devote more time to the human aspect of patient care. It will be essential to invest in the training of healthcare professionals to make the most of AI's potential and address the ethical and social challenges it poses.

Dr. Giuseppe Rotolo

The Art and Science of Source Selection: A Guide to Quality Medical Research

Introduction

Artificial Intelligence: An Indispensable Ally in Modern Medicine

The explosion of medical literature has created a paradox: on the one hand, we have access to an unprecedented amount of information, but on the other hand, physicians find themselves navigating a sea of data, risking drowning. Artificial Intelligence (AI) presents itself as a compass in this ocean of information, offering increasingly sophisticated tools to:

Dr. Giuseppe Rotolo

Targeted searches: Artificial Intelligence (AI) algorithms can rapidly analyze vast databases, identifying the most relevant studies for a specific clinical question. This allows physicians to save precious time and focus on interpreting the results.

Dr. Giuseppe Rotolo

Evidence synthesis: Artificial Intelligence (AI) can synthesize evidence from multiple studies, providing physicians with a clear and concise overview of the state of the art on a given topic.

Risk prediction: Artificial Intelligence (AI) models can be trained on large datasets to predict the risk of developing certain diseases or experiencing complications from specific therapies.

Treatment personalization: Artificial Intelligence (AI) can help personalize treatments based on a patient's genetic, clinical, and socioeconomic characteristics.

Dr. Giuseppe Rotolo

Diagnostic support: Artificial Intelligence (AI) can support physicians in making diagnoses by analyzing medical images (X-rays, CT scans, MRIs) and identifying patterns that may escape the human eye.

Physicians with autism spectrum disorder often possess exceptional analytical skills and a capacity for concentration, making them particularly suited to professions that require a high level of precision. However, they may encounter difficulties in social interactions and communication. AI can offer valuable support in this context.

Assisted communication: Chatbots and virtual assistants can facilitate communication between the physician and the patient, providing language support and managing simpler interactions.

Data visualization: Artificial Intelligence (AI) can present clinical data in a clear and visual manner, facilitating understanding and communication of information.

Dr. Giuseppe Rotolo

communication

ai
data
sup
interactions

autism evaluating language
information
difficulties pressed
level concentration professions
disorder capacity

particularly: 1

Dr. Giuseppe Rotolo

What are the benefits of approaching a book through its keywords?

Nodal Learning: A New Paradigm for Knowledge Acquisition

Providing keywords at the beginning of each chapter represents a significant innovation in the field of education, bringing us closer to a more intuitive and natural learning model. This approach, defined as "nodal" or "networked," is based on creating connections between concepts, rather than on a linear sequence of information.

Why is Nodal Learning Effective?

Alignment with neurobiology: Our brain does not store information in an isolated manner, but organizes it into semantic networks. Each new concept is linked to pre-existing ones, creating a complex and dynamic architecture. Nodal learning, by providing an overview and reference points, facilitates the creation of these neural connections.

Cognitive flexibility: This approach adapts to different learning styles, allowing each reader to build

Dr. Giuseppe Rotolo

their own conceptual map. This is particularly advantageous for healthcare professionals, who often have to deal with complex situations and require flexible thinking.

Better retention: Information linked to a network of concepts is more easily retrievable from memory. This is because the brain can follow different paths to access information, making memory more resistant to forgetting.

Facilitation of problem-solving: Nodal learning encourages viewing problems from different perspectives, fostering creativity and innovation in solving clinical problems.

Concrete examples of application in the healthcare field

Pathology: Creating conceptual maps that connect symptoms, clinical signs, causes, and possible diagnoses of a disease facilitates differential diagnosis.

Epidemiology: Visualizing risk factors, pathogenic mechanisms, and the consequences of a disease as an interconnected network helps to understand the complexity of chronic diseases.

Dr. Giuseppe Rotolo

Pathology: Creating maps connect symptoms, clinical signs

How

Creating maps that connect symptoms and clinical signs involves a systematic approach to understanding the relationships between various health indicators. This process typically starts with the collection of data from patient histories, clinical examinations, and diagnostic tests. By analyzing this data, healthcare professionals can identify patterns and correlations, which can be visualized in the form of maps or diagrams. These maps help in diagnosing conditions, predicting disease progression, and tailoring treatment plans by providing a clear visual representation of how different symptoms and signs are interrelated.

Epidemiology: Visualizing risk factors, pathogenic mechanisms, and the consequences of a disease as an interconnected network helps to understand the complexity of chronic diseases.

Dr. Giuseppe Rotolo

Origin

Epidemiology, the study of how diseases affect the health and illness of populations, has its roots in the early 19th century. The term itself is derived from the Greek words "epi" (upon), "demos" (people), and "logos" (study), reflecting its focus on the distribution and determinants of health-related states. One of the pivotal figures in the development of epidemiology was John Snow, who is often referred to as the father of modern epidemiology. In the mid-1800s, he famously traced a cholera outbreak in London to a contaminated water pump, illustrating the importance of environmental factors in disease transmission.

The visualization of risk factors and disease spread has evolved significantly since then, particularly with advancements in statistical methods and technology. Tools such as Geographic Information Systems (GIS) have enhanced the ability to map and analyze health data spatially. This visualization helps identify patterns and correlations, making it easier to communicate ...

Epidemiology: Visualizing risk factors, disease

Dr. Giuseppe Rotolo

Continuous updating: The healthcare profession requires continuous updating. Nodal learning allows new knowledge to be integrated into the pre-existing network, facilitating continuous updating.

Clinical decision making: By linking symptoms, test results, and therapeutic options, nodal learning supports the physician in making informed and effective clinical decisions.

Effective communication: The ability to visualize and communicate information clearly and concisely is essential in the doctor-patient relationship. Nodal learning helps to develop this skill.

Conclusions

The nodal approach represents a significant evolution in the education of health sciences. By offering a more natural and intuitive way of learning, this method can improve understanding, retention, and application of knowledge. Investing in this type of education means investing in the training of more competent and prepared healthcare professionals to face the challenges of the ever-evolving healthcare world.

Possible future developments

Nodal learning holds great promise for providing more effective and personalized training, particularly for autistic physicians. However, current Artificial Intelligence (AI) interfaces often present information in a linear format without

Dr. Giuseppe Rotolo

knowledge graphs, hindering the full potential of this approach. Various groups are working to bridge this gap.

Dr. Giuseppe Rotolo

Stress reduction: Automations and support systems can reduce the workload and perceived stress of physicians, improving their quality of life

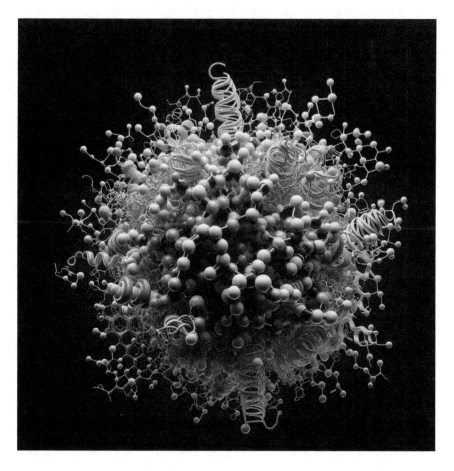

Dr. Giuseppe Rotolo

Automations reduce workload perceived stress physicians

How

Automations streamline repetitive tasks, allowing physicians to focus more on patient care rather than administrative duties. By handling scheduling, billing, and data entry, these systems minimize the time spent on non-clinical activities, which can lead to burnout. Additionally, automations can enhance accuracy in documentation and reduce the likelihood of errors, further alleviating stress. As a result, physicians experience a more manageable workload, contributing to improved job satisfaction and overall well-being.

Dr. Giuseppe Rotolo

Autistic physicians bring a unique skill set to healthcare, characterized by exceptional attention to detail, logical reasoning, and a deep focus. However, the demanding nature of the medical profession can exacerbate challenges often associated with autism spectrum disorder (ASD), such as sensory overload, social interactions, and the need for routine. Chronic stress, a common occupational hazard in healthcare, can be particularly detrimental to autistic physicians due to their heightened sensitivity to stimuli.

To optimize the well-being and performance of autistic physicians, a strategic approach is required. The integration of automation and support systems can significantly mitigate the stressors inherent in medical practice. By automating routine tasks, such as data entry, appointment scheduling, and electronic health record documentation, physicians can allocate more cognitive resources to complex patient care decisions. Moreover, these technologies can facilitate communication and collaboration, addressing challenges in social interactions often experienced by autistic individuals.

Creating a structured and predictable work environment is essential for autistic physicians. Automation can contribute to this by standardizing procedures and reducing unexpected interruptions. Additionally, incorporating sensory accommodations, like noise-canceling equipment or adjustable lighting, can significantly enhance the work environment for individuals with sensory sensitivities.

Dr. Giuseppe Rotolo

As mentioned elsewhere in the book, keywords are displayed in different colors for readers of the electronic version. Unfortunately, readers of the print version will not be able to see these colors."

"Keywords are highlighted in color for digital readers, but this feature is not available in the print edition.

Beyond stress reduction, investing in automation and support systems for autistic physicians offers broader benefits.

Dr. Giuseppe Rotolo

stress reduction automation support for autistic physicians

How

Stress reduction automation support for autistic physicians involves the integration of technology to help manage stress and enhance well-being in a clinical environment. This can include tools like scheduling software that optimizes work hours to prevent burnout, or apps that provide mindfulness exercises and relaxation techniques tailored to individual needs. Additionally, automated reminders for breaks and self-care activities can help maintain a balanced workflow. By leveraging these technologies, autistic physicians can create a more supportive work environment that accommodates their unique challenges and promotes mental health.

By optimizing their work-life balance and job satisfaction, we can increase retention rates and build a more stable healthcare workforce. Furthermore, reducing physician burnout can lead to improved patient outcomes, as less stressed clinicians are better equipped to provide compassionate and effective care.

A holistic approach to supporting autistic physicians is crucial. This includes not only the implementation of

Dr. Giuseppe Rotolo

technology but also the provision of training, mentorship, and a workplace culture that values diversity and inclusion. By fostering a supportive environment, healthcare organizations can unlock the full potential of autistic physicians and contribute to a more equitable and high-performing healthcare system.

Ultimately, the goal is to create a healthcare environment where autistic physicians can thrive. By investing in automation, support systems, and a culture of inclusivity, we can help to ensure that these exceptional individuals have the tools and support they need to excel in their careers.

The challenges of discerning reliable sources from unreliable ones

Dr. Giuseppe Rotolo

How

stress reduction automation support for autistic physicians

Stress reduction automation support for autistic physicians involves the integration of technology to help manage stress and enhance well-being in a clinical environment. This can include tools like scheduling software that optimizes work hours to prevent burnout, or apps that provide mindfulness exercises and relaxation techniques tailored to individual needs. Additionally, automated reminders for breaks and self-care activities can help maintain a balanced workflow. By leveraging these technologies, autistic physicians can create a more supportive work environment that accommodates their unique challenges and promotes mental health.

Dr. Giuseppe Rotolo

The importance of evidence-based medicine

Expanding on the Importance of Quality Sources in Medical Research

Dr. Giuseppe Rotolo

Patient safety: Relying on inaccurate information can lead to misdiagnosis, inappropriate treatment, and adverse events.

Scientific advancement: High-quality research builds upon previous findings, ensuring that medical knowledge grows in a reliable and cumulative manner.

Access to a vast array of high-quality scientific articles is essential for accurate diagnoses and effective treatments. Autistic physicians, equipped with AI tools, can overcome

Dr. Giuseppe Rotolo

potential challenges related to social interactions or information processing and achieve exceptional professional performance. By leveraging AI's ability to process large amounts of data and identify relevant information, autistic physicians can contribute significantly to the medical field, both clinically and academically

Dr. Giuseppe Rotolo

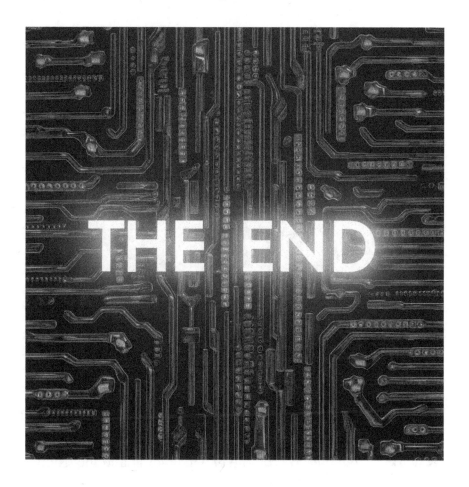

This book explored the role of Artificial Intelligence (AI) in supporting medical professionals, particularly those on the autism spectrum. It provided a comprehensive overview of the challenges and opportunities that Artificial Intelligence (AI) presents for autistic doctors.

The book highlighted how Artificial Intelligence (AI) can be a powerful tool to improve the lives of autistic doctors. It can

Dr. Giuseppe Rotolo

help overcome social and sensory barriers, enhance efficiency and productivity, and contribute to mental well-being.

Autistic Doctors International (ADI), an association of 1,000 physicians, exemplifies how the autistic medical community is working together to promote understanding and inclusion.

 Link: www.bit.ly/AD-I

Autistic Doctors International (ADI)

Do you identify as autistic and have a medical degree?

Dr. Giuseppe Rotolo

The experience of one autistic doctor, shared in the book, offers a valuable firsthand account of the challenges and successes that autistic doctors may encounter.

The book concludes with a message of hope and optimism. Artificial Intelligence (AI) has the potential to transform the medical profession and create a more inclusive and supportive environment for autistic doctors. With continued advancements in Artificial Intelligence (AI) technology and the support of the autistic medical community, a future can be envisioned where autistic doctors can thrive and reach their full potential.

Key takeaways from the conclusion:

Artificial Intelligence (AI) is a powerful tool that can improve the lives of autistic doctors.

Autistic Doctors International (ADI) is an example of how the autistic medical community is working together to promote understanding and inclusion.

The experience of one autistic doctor offers valuable insights into the challenges and successes that autistic doctors may encounter.

The future of medicine is promising for autistic doctors, thanks to Artificial Intelligence (AI) and the support of the community.

Dr. Giuseppe Rotolo

Call to action

The book encourages readers to learn more about Artificial Intelligence (AI) and its potential to improve the medical profession. It also invites autistic doctors to join Autistic Doctors International (ADI) and other support organizations to share their experiences and promote inclusion.

Expanded Conclusion

This book has merely scratched the surface of the vast potential of Artificial Intelligence (AI) to support medical professionals, especially those on the autism spectrum. As we've seen, Artificial Intelligence (AI) can be a powerful tool for overcoming challenges and enhancing the abilities of autistic doctors.

The journey doesn't end here

In the following volumes of this series, we will delve deeper into the intricacies of cognitive functions, such as working memory. We will explore how working memory, a crucial cognitive process for both autistic and non-autistic individuals, can be assessed and enhanced. Furthermore, we

Dr. Giuseppe Rotolo

will investigate personalized Artificial Intelligence (AI) interfaces designed to cater to the unique cognitive styles and needs of different individuals.

Choosing the right Artificial Intelligence (AI) tool is paramount

We will explore the various Artificial Intelligence (AI) models available and discuss the factors to consider when selecting the most suitable Artificial Intelligence (AI) for specific tasks. From natural language processing to machine learning, we will examine how these technologies can be harnessed to create tailored solutions for healthcare professionals.

The future of Artificial Intelligence (AI) in medicine is bright. As Artificial Intelligence (AI) technology continues to evolve, we can expect even more innovative applications that will revolutionize the way we practice medicine. By understanding the unique strengths and challenges of autistic doctors, we can develop Artificial Intelligence (AI) tools that empower them to reach their full potential and contribute meaningfully to the healthcare field.

Dr. Giuseppe Rotolo

Continue the conversation Join the ongoing discussion about Artificial Intelligence (AI) and autism in medicine

Share your experiences, insights, and ideas on our online forums and social media channels.

Explore further: Delve deeper into the topics covered in this book by consulting additional resources and conducting your own research.

Embrace the future: Be open to new technologies and embrace the opportunities that Artificial Intelligence (AI) presents.

By working together, we can create a future where Artificial Intelligence (AI) and human expertise complement each other, leading to improved patient care and a more inclusive healthcare system.

This book has laid the groundwork for a future where Artificial Intelligence (AI) and human expertise seamlessly collaborate to enhance healthcare. We have explored the unique challenges and opportunities that Artificial Intelligence (AI) presents for autistic doctors and the broader medical community.

Dr. Giuseppe Rotolo

As we look ahead, it is imperative to establish standardized guidelines for training Artificial Intelligence (AI) models tailored to the needs of healthcare professionals, regardless of their neurodiversity. By creating a repository of best practices and ethical considerations, we can accelerate the development of Artificial Intelligence (AI) tools that are both effective and inclusive.

 Lonk: www.bit.ly/w-as

The World Autism Summit 2024 served as a catalyst for these discussions, bringing together experts from various fields to share their insights and experiences. The collective wisdom gained from this summit can inform the development of these guidelines and ensure that Artificial Intelligence (AI)

Dr. Giuseppe Rotolo

technologies benefit all members of the healthcare community.

In conclusion, the potential of Artificial Intelligence (AI) to revolutionize healthcare is vast. By fostering collaboration between researchers, clinicians, and individuals on the autism spectrum, we can create a future where Artificial Intelligence (AI) serves as a powerful ally, enhancing the abilities of healthcare professionals and improving patient outcomes.

Dr. Giuseppe Rotolo

Call to action

Contribute to the knowledge base: Share your expertise and experiences to help shape the future of Artificial Intelligence (AI) in healthcare.

> **Advocate for ethical Artificial Intelligence (AI):** Promote the development and implementation of Artificial Intelligence (AI) technologies that are fair, transparent, and accountable.

> **Support ongoing research:** Continue to fund and support research that explores the intersection of Artificial Intelligence (AI) and autism.

Together, we can build a more inclusive and equitable future for all.

One aspect often overlooked in technological advancements is the importance of design. The visual and sensory elements of technology can significantly impact user experience, especially for individuals with sensory sensitivities. That is why we have carefully curated the design of this book, ensuring that it is accessible to a wide range of readers,

Dr. Giuseppe Rotolo

including those with autism or other sensory processing differences.

As we move forward, it is crucial to prioritize inclusive design in all Artificial Intelligence (AI) applications. By considering the needs of neurodivergent individuals from the outset, we can create technologies that are truly beneficial for everyone.

Let us work together to build a future where Artificial Intelligence (AI) and human ingenuity coexist harmoniously, empowering individuals of all abilities to reach their full potential.

Dr. Giuseppe Rotolo

www.ingramcontent.com/pod-product-compliance
Lightning Source LLC
La Vergne TN
LVHW051335050326
832903LV00031B/3547